THE SUN OF GOODNESS NEVER SETS

Compiled by: Sr. Annette Thottakara fdcc

BookLeaf
Publishing

THE SUN OF GOODNESS NEVER SETS ©
2023 Sr. Annette Thottakara

Presentation by *BookLeaf Publishing*

Web: www.bookleafpub.com

E-mail: info@bookleafpub.com

ISBN: 9789358315417

First edition 2023

Whatever one does for

the welfare of another

turns into blessings for oneself!

CONTENTS

Dedication

Yours Gratefully

Blessing : Rt. Rev. Dr. Bishop James
Anaparambil, Alappuzha

Introduction : Alive! Aware!! Active!!!

Part I : They Took the Road Less Traveled

Part II : Environment, Food & Health Are Triplets

Part III : On the Ladder of Literacy & Learning

Part IV : My Home, My Castle

End Note : Forward Hoi!

*"Life is better when you are happy.
Life is at its best when other people
are happy because of you."*

DEDICATED

TO THE GOOD SAMARITANS WHO READILY
POUR LOVE'S HEALING BALM
ON THE WOUNDED & THE BROKEN HEARTED,
TO THE CANOSSIAN CONGREGATION THAT
NURTURED ME
FOR THE LAST SIXTY YEARS.

YOURS GRATEFULLY

God comes to find us in the midst of our sorrows, when we are trapped by disappointments, betrayed by our presumptions about ourselves and our achievements. In the following pages, the reader will find God's great plan of finding His children in the depth of distress and lifting them to love and life through the superhuman deeds of a few ordinary humans who, by their altruistic deeds, proved that they are a cut above the rest. As I present this narration to you, reader, I bow in thanks to:

: *The First Mover Unmoved* who *moved* the hearts of a few munificent residents of our planet to take the road less traveled and did their *Little-Great-Bits* and wove threads of joy and hope into some turbulent hearts and helped them to spin their individual destinies.

: Rt. Rev. Dr. James Anaparambil, Bishop of Alappuzha, for his words of Blessing.

: The print and the social media that found it appropriate to proclaim to the world the bounteous deeds of these over-generous women and men that *moved* me to compile the heroic and benevolent acts of theirs that caught my attention.

: All the sisters of my community for their wholehearted support and help.

: Prof. Kunjannam Andrews, my teacher and Prof. Agnes Mathew, my colleague, who found time to read through the text and for their valuable corrections and suggestions.

: Sr. Elizabeth Nooranmakal, St. Joseph's Convent, Shri. Manoj Peter, St. Antony's Press, Alappuzha, for the inspiring cover design.

: The *BookLeaf Publishers*, Delhi and their editor, my niece Ivy Thomas, for their timely help.

: All the readers who will find time to glance through the following pages. Thank You All.

Sr.Annette Thottakara

We are defined not by our limitations but by the intention God has for us in creating us.

MESSAGE

Shakespeare's dirge "The evil that men do lives after them; the good is oft interred with their bones" however moving, falls short of the wooing words of Jesus: "Let your light so shine before men, that they may see your good works and glorify your Father who is in heaven." (Mt. 5:14-16.)

In the following pages, Sr. Annette Thottakara fdcc showcases a few golden leaves - described as glow worms - who from their ordinariness and littleness, gave willingly more than their share, even life itself, for the benefit of the non-descript others and nobodies. They proved that incredible goodness reveals itself in the face of unimaginable tragedies. The author honestly writes that she is not pampering the readers with imaginative stories or cogitations; rather she is only compiling potpourris - often surprising - originating from benevolent comrades of our techno-gen and new-gen era. For that matter, her sources are well-authenticated and documented with true names, places and time. It is heartening to note that our hustle and technology-overloaded culture has not blown out the innate and deep-rooted goodness that gushes forth resiliently in humans in the face of tragedies and grief. While many are driven by carpe diem and dreaming of living in the lap of luxury, some startle us with their readiness to give up even the little they have for the benefit of co-humans and weave their days in wiping away the tears from their fellow beings.

Let more of these deeds of altruism and amity shine before the world and inspire many more glow worms to express openly their empathy and compassion for the benefit of humanity. Sr. Annette is saying it well: goodness diffuses itself.

November 2023   Bishop James Anaparambil
                                                    Alappuzha

ALIVE! . . . AWARE!! . . . ACTIVE!!!

The setting sun asked: "Now that I am retiring, who will take up the work of dispelling darkness and lighting up the world?" For a while, the whole world stood aghast and speechless for obvious reasons. Then a little glow worm broke the grim silence and ventured: "I shall, as much as it is possible for me." In the following pages, the reader will find a few tiny glow worms who, driven by the desire to dispel the darkness caused by illiteracy, ignorance, accidents, illnesses, hunger, homelessness and exploitation by ivory tower dwellers, took the road less traveled to light up the little space around them and that made a positive difference in the lives of the disadvantaged in their area. These glow worms believed that only the impossible is worth doing and punched above their weight and sowed seeds of growth, changed thought patterns, nurtured development, powered the vision for a better future and transformed the lives of a few co-humans living in the tiniest corners of our mighty planet. They did more than was possible for them to light the lamp of hope and well-being in the hearts of the lost and the least, the neglected and the needy, the unknown entities living on the margins. Hence, they rewrote the stories of a few underprivileged and shaped for them a future better than they had dreamt of.

The compiler of this volume hereby declares that the contents of the book titled *The Sun of Goodness Never Sets* are not the fruits of her imagination but real down-to-earth ways some Good Samaritans in flesh and blood endangered even their lives and limbs to help a few in distress, whose humanitarian and altruistic deeds found a place in some newspaper columns. Inspiration to collect such golden deeds of these other-oriented women and men came from Harish Nanjappa (26), a highly placed and highly paid techie, who met with an accident and lay bleeding on a road in Bangalore. Just before he flew to the Great Beyond, when the police reached to pick him up, with his last breath he said, "I want to donate my organs," and said goodbye to our planet.

This volume contains four parts. **Part I: They Took the Road Less Traveled** has two sections. Section 1: chronicles the heroic deeds of a few who readily parted with parts of their body - Organ Donation - to save the lives of those in danger of death. Section 2 of Part I brings to light the life-saving mission of some brave, other-centered heroes and heroines who stuck their necks out, put themselves in danger of death and succeeded to pull away their co-humans from the jaws of death. Ajay Krishnan (20), IV Year Industrial Engineering student at the College of Engineering and Technology, Kariavattam,

TVPM, donated his bone marrow to Ajay (12), son of C. Unnikrishnan, Thekkeplathottathu House, Parasala, TVPM. It was a special donation on two counts. 1. The generous donor and the grateful receiver have not seen each other and were absolute strangers. 2. Donating bone marrow to anyone other than a blood relation is an unusual case. The donation was from Ajay to Ajay. Pre-teen Ajay, the receiver, was suffering from a blood-related illness known as Aplastic Anaemia, a rare and serious blood condition that occurs when a person's bone marrow cannot produce enough new blood cells for the body to work normally. In 2015, Ajay, the donor, registered his name at the *Dathri Stem Cells Donors' Registry* and the donation took place via the Registry. When junior Ajay's need arose, senior Ajay was contacted and he was more than willing to help out. Without much delay, the bone marrow transplant took place at Apollo Hospital, Chennai. According to the Registry, Ajay is the first unrelated bone marrow donor in Kerala and the third in India. It was described as the rarest of rare donations by social media. (Manorama, 15.10. 2016) Section 2 brings to the attention of the reader the heroism of a few caring altruists who wagered their own lives or better put their lives on the chopping block and carried back to life a few co-humans who were almost on the point of bidding good-bye to our planet.

Rishikesh Narayan Singh's father is in the transport business in Bengaluru. His brother, who is a software engineer at Wipro, also stays in Bengaluru. But Rishikesh, a 26-year-old Research Scholar in Patna, was not lured by power and pelf and decided to stay back to serve the famished poor of Bihar. After launching Gyan-deep Book Bank, an initiative to donate books to underprivileged kids, Rishikesh vowed not to let anyone in his neighborhood go hungry. "Initially, we plan to feed at least 100 famished people who do not get a proper meal. We will start from Ashok Rajpath near Patna Medical College and Hospital and cover up to Patna junction, where there are many people who do not get adequate food. At the same time, we will ensure that only genuinely needy people get the food as we do not intend to encourage *bhiksha-vriti*" (begging as a lifestyle), he added. From where did he get this idea of Roti Bank? "Actually, the trend was started by Dabbawallahs in Mumbai in 2015. I watched on YouTube how the Dabbawallahs ensured proper food for the needy. This gave me the idea to start a Roti Bank here in the State capital," Rishikesh reminisced. **Part II: Environment, Food & Health** are Siamese Triplets narrates the life-saving services of a few benevolent humans like Rishikesh Narayan, who heard the mournful cry of empty stomachs and did what they could to lessen their hunger pangs and consequently gave an upward push to their health index. (DNA, 05.05.2017)

The mission of a few philanthropists who took to heart the instruction of our Mahatma, "If we want to reach real peace in this world, we should start educating children," and did their share to spread literacy and learning among the penniless ones in street corners or shop verandas, is brought to light in **Part III: On the Ladder of Literacy and Learning**. The idea to open a school dawned on Rajesh (41) during a morning walk along the river when he saw some children weeding and collecting flowers. "I asked them which school they go to and they looked at me in wonder and did not answer. It had not occurred to me before that not every child has access to a school," said Rajesh, who runs a grocery shop across the street from the Yamuna Vihar Metro Station. This special school that offers free basic education to the children of the local laborers and farmers has no desks, no chairs. The metro railway bridge 10 meters overhead is the roof of the school. The blackboards are rectangles painted on the wall of the adjacent station. Together with his friend Laxmi Chandra, a retired teacher, Rajesh started classes under the metro bridge for two hours in the morning on weekdays. After the government enforced the Right to Education Act (2009) which guarantees free schooling for children between the ages of 6 and 14, Rajesh decided to focus on preparing the children for admission to school and helping them to cope with the curriculum. The students, who now number more than 70, sit on foam mats and are taught English alphabets, mathematics, multiplication tables, geometry, history and more, and as they recite numbers and alphabets or what has been taught previously, trains rumble overhead and traffic rolls past a few meters away. "These are children who cannot afford private tuition to help them with their school homework," Chandra said. Rajesh initially bore the entire cost of providing the children with textbooks, pencils and exercise books. Later, good-hearted people who heard about the school began dropping off supplies, sometimes anonymously. "One man came with 60 school bags once," he said. "He would not tell me his name or other details about him. He said none of that mattered as long as the children got a decent education." Rajesh has to battle constantly to get parents to send their children to his classes for a couple of hours each day. All it takes for a parent is to enroll the child in a government school, which also provides free lunch. Most parents of the children that Rajesh teaches are reluctant to do even that. Being squatters, they have no residency papers and are reluctant to interact with the authorities for fear that it might draw attention to their illegally constructed huts. (sbhattacharya@thenational.ae, Suryatapa Bhattacharya, 15. 04. 2013)

"Life's persistent and the most urgent question is: 'What are you doing for others?'" After reading in Malayala Manorama about the miserable plight of Ashok Kumari and her children, a roofless family that made the premises of T.D. Govt. Medical College, Alappuzha, their home, the above question which Martin Luther King Jr. (1929-1964) asked more than half a century ago, rang a do-something-bell in the heart of Sunil Joseph Vanchickal, Thathampally, Alappuzha. The milk of human kindness spilt over from his heart and on listening to his inner voice, Sunil swung into action and decided that before celebrating the birth of Jesus the Homeless One in a stable, he would provide a home for the present-day homeless Jesuses. He bought three and a half cents of land with a house in Kanjikkuzhi, Alappuzha and presented the same to Ashok Kumari and her children. On Christmas day, 25 December 2016, they left the hospital premises, which was their home till then, where they had spent their days without any privacy or protection. The key to the new house was handed over to

Ashok Kumari by the then Minister G. Sudhakaran, who requested the panchayat members to see to the continued security of the family.

Part IV - My Home, My Castle, narrates how a person's thatched hut is more valuable to them than Burj Khalifa or Taj Mahal. Therefore, it is a great act of munificence to help a person own his/her own Windsor Castle. (Manorama, 27.12.2016) By their intelligence and grace, their courage and good cheer, these noble humanitarians proved that they were exceptional lovers of humanity. They did not wait for the window of opportunity to open before them but forced open the windows and found opportunity waiting for them. They were led by their dreams and were prepared not to be pushed out by problems. Even when they lacked resources, they depended on their resourcefulness to make the lives of those on the periphery less burdensome and more liveable. The contents of this volume, placed in chronological order, owe a debt of gratitude to a few trustworthy newspapers that the compiler happened to read. It is not even .00000001% of the golden deeds of the multitudes of the angels of unconditional love and dedication who toil to wipe the tears of the forgotten ones of our land. It has been compiled with the fervent hope that these benignant humans who have gone before us will find some ardent followers.

Endnote:

A man dug a well in his property and pasted a notice that no one should take water from the well; only his family could have it. The well, however, was dry. He approached a man of God who told him that there would be no water unless he shared the water with his neighbors. Then he posted a notice to the effect that his neighbors could take water from the well after sunset; he and his family would have it during the day. On the following day, the water failed to appear. After the sun retired having done his duty for the day, the people gathered around the well with their empty vessels. Bingo! Fresh sparkling water gushed from the spring beneath and water rose up to the brim. They filled their vessels and went back home dancing, but when the morning came, the well was dry. Then the owner was forced to put up another notice in the morning. Let the readers' imagination help them deduce the contents of the last notice. Our lives will overflow with wellness when we extend a helping hand for the well-being of other human beings. Giving without measure is the measure of humaneness and the road to happiness.

Sr. Annette Thottakara

Somebody did a golden deed,
Somebody helped a friend in need
Somebody sang a beautiful song,
Somebody smiled the whole day long.
Somebody thought 'tis sweet to live,
Somebody said 'I am glad to give'.
Somebody fought a valiant fight,
Somebody lived to shield the right.
Was that Somebody You? . . . You? . .

(Unknown Author)

I

THEY TOOK THE ROAD LESS TRAVELED

PART I: ORGAN DONATION

If life is the most precious thing we have in this world, love is the most excitingly wonderful thing in life. A life without love is as good as death. We always have a second chance with almost everything except life. Love infiltrates every fiber of our being and every aspect of our daily lives and it is the most important factor for our mental and physical health. In the first part of this volume, the reader gets a chance to learn about a few ardent lovers of life who, on the face of death, offered the elixir of life to others - Harish Nanjappa (26) appearing in the next paragraph did exactly that - and about a few bereaved families consenting to the harvesting of the organs of the dear departed to help other patients waiting for fitting organs to replace their non-functioning ones. This part also includes the heroic stories of a few who sacrificed their lives to rescue others in danger, Noushad of Kozhikode being a supreme example. Though these lovers of humanity have said goodbye to our planet, they continue to live in the hearts of their beneficiaries and those who have known them in life.

As the Clock of Life Ticked Inexorably. . .

"His Body Cut into Two, Man Makes Organ Donation Wish" (Bangalore, sp. correspondent). This was the front page banner headline that appeared in the Deccan Herald and in many other newspapers in South India on 17 February 2016. Around 8.30 am on Tuesday 16 February, while Harish Nanjappa (26), a resident of Gubbi in Tumakuru, was riding to work, a lorry brushed past his motorcycle and Harish lost control over his two-wheeler, went under the lorry and his body was ripped apart.

According to Neelamangala police: "At Thippegondanahalli, near Neelamangala (NH 4), Bengaluru, a lorry carrying sugar bags tried to overtake Harish's bike, the lorry accidentally touched the bike, causing Harish to lose his balance. He fell under the wheels of the lorry and his body was severed. His body was cut into two, and Harish was found lying on the road, bleeding profusely and pleading for help." The severely injured victim was hanging between life and death when the police ambulance reached the site. As the clock of his life ticked on feebly, Harish managed to utter a few words to the ambulance staff: "If any organ in my body can be donated, please donate it." Harish's last words! The police shifted him to a nearby hospital, where minutes later, he was declared dead. "It is unbelievable that someone whose body is sliced into two, masters courage to inform the police of his wish to donate his organs. It's astounding how a man who was split into two and lying on the road was able to think with such clarity. It's unheard of!", commented Dr. Bhujang Shetty, Chairman and Managing Director, Narayana Nethralaya, Bengaluru. "Only his corneas have been harvested; sadly, his other organs could not be taken since they were badly damaged in the accident," added Dr. Shetty. "It was heroic of Harish to think of donating his organs to help others even as he lay in the middle of a road," Dr. Ajit Benedict Rayan, Medical Director, HOSMAT Hospital, said. *Dear Harish, may your sky-high other-centeredness inspire us to move on the path of altruism and service.* (Deccan Herald, 17.02.2016)

Good-bye to Life! Welcome to Life!!

After giving new life and light to five of his fellow beings, who were complete strangers to him, Biju winged his way to the next world. Due to high blood pressure, Biju collapsed at about 05.30 am on 26 August 2016 and was admitted to the nearby hospital, from where he was shifted to Lourdes Hospital, Ernakulam (EKM), for better care. Due to brain hemorrhage, the brain death of Padathuruthil Biju (47), Paravoor Madaplathuruth Labour Jn., was confirmed by the doctors. Though immersed in an ocean of sorrow, his family members expressed their willingness to donate his organs. So Biju continues to live on! His heart was transplanted into a person from Fort Kochi who was under treatment in Amrita Hospital, EKM. One of the kidneys was given to Vimala (52), who was being treated at Lourdes Hospital by Dr. H. Krishna Moorthy. The other kidney was donated to Anil Kumar from Kottayam, Kodimatha, under the guidance of K. P. Jayakumar, HoD of Nephrology. Eyes were shifted to the clinic by Dr. Tony Fernandez. Biju has left behind his wife Sindhu and Bisiya, a Higher Secondary student and Neha, studying in Std. III. (Manorama, 27.08.2016)

"Your organ could be someone's missing piece."

A Great Heart with Two Ready Hands

Sudhil Kumar L (34) was on the Huballi-Dharwad highway returning to the city with friends after an exciting trip to Goa, when he spotted a jeep that had lost control and hit a tree. The onlookers stood paralyzed and did not move an inch to help those stuck in the vehicle. Sudhil took charge of the situation, helped the two injured passengers out of the crushed jeep and ensured that they reached the hospital safely. "When we approached the vehicle, we found that the two passengers were bleeding heavily. We managed to get them on the ground with difficulty and gave them water and first aid that we had in our car. The injured persons were officials from Konkan Railway who were returning home after their night shift. Deprived of sleep, they lost control of the vehicle," said Sudhil, an IT professional. The compassion and humanity that Sudhil displayed have put him on the list of 40 nominees for the Columbia Asia Good Samaritan Awards in association with the Times of India (ToI). It was Sudhil's will to make a difference in the lives of fellow humans that turned him into an ambassador for the Good Samaritan Initiative (GSI). The GSI by Columbia Asia Hospital, in association with Bengaluru traffic police and the ToI, seeks to recognize and award such selfless acts. (ToI, 25.07.2016, Deepika, Burli@times grcup.com)

Hearts & Hands Moved in Unison

After an attack of paralysis, Suresh (10), the son of Soma Sanglala, hailing from Fatepura in Gujarat, was treated at the Civil Hospital in Rajkot for several days. When the hospital expenses became too heavy for his almost empty purse to handle, Soma, who worked as a farm laborer in the neighboring Junagadh District, decided to leave the hospital along with his wife and their ailing son. They reached Rajkot Central Bus Depot with, agonizing hearts, an empty purse, and hungry stomachs while their sick son was hanging between life and death. Nishant Vermora, Manager of the bus depot, said: "They were confused and unsure about what to do with their son who was almost on the point of death. They had no money to purchase even bus tickets, let alone hire an ambulance to carry their boy home which is nearly 400 km. from the bus depot. They asked some passengers for money to purchase the bus tickets. When we came to know about the sad situation, we called the ambulance 108. The medical staff of the ambulance declared Suresh dead." A few Good Samaritans at the depot, including the staff, small shopkeepers and passengers waiting for their bus to continue their journey, decided to help out the couple in dire need. "In a matter of a few hours, around Rs.10,000/- was raised and handed over to the couple to hire an ambulance to carry their dear departed son home and perform the last rites," said Vermora, with a sense of satisfaction after having helped the parents in distress. Verily, the Sun of Goodness shines brightly in some hearts! (DH 14.09.2016, Rajkot: PTI)

> *"The happiest people are not those who get more but those who give more."* (H.J. Brown Jr.)

******

Deceased Karthik is Alive

On 21 September 2016, Karthik Banakar fell 50 feet from the Hebbal flyover, which resulted in injuries all over his body. His friends rushed him to Baptist Hospital, Hebbal, Bengaluru, where he received initial treatment. "Later, we shifted him to Sakra World Hospital, where we were told that he had sustained critical injuries in the brain and in the spinal cord. He was kept on ventilation for three days. Despite all the attempts by the doctors for almost a week, we lost our son," said Mrutyunjaya Banakar, the grief-stricken father of Karthik when his son was declared brain dead. "While waiting for our son's recovery, we came to know from the hospital authorities that there are several critical patients waiting for an organ and all of them can get a new lease of life if they receive a healthy organ. We know the high mortality rate due to the low availability of organs in our State, so we decided to donate Karthik's organs. I wanted him to serve people this way," said Banakar, even as he mourned the unexpected departure of his son. A green corridor was created in the evening to carry the heart to MS Narayan Heart Centre. A team of doctors performed a successful heart transplant on a 45-year-old man from Chikkaballapur who was suffering from dilated cardiomyopathy and had been waiting for a heart transplant for three years. His liver has been kept at the Health Care Global (HCG) Hospital, where Karthik was admitted. His kidneys and corneas were donated as well. (ToI, 29. 09. 2016)

"What does one person give to another? He gives of himself, he gives of his life." (E.Fromm)

******

Greater Love than Noushad's . . .?

Nearly a year after the auto-rickshaw driver Noushad P. died a heroic death trying to save the lives of two migrant sanitation workers, his colleagues were looking for the Best Auto-rickshaw Driver in Kozhikode to honor his memory. "We want to commemorate the supreme sacrifice made by Noushad, the young auto-rickshaw driver," Gafoor Puthiyangadi, General Convenor of the initiative and a functionary of the HMS Auto-Rickshaw Drivers Association, told The Hindu. "By instituting the Best Auto-Rickshaw Driver Award, we are urging others to emulate Noushad's humaneness and compassion," he added. Thomas Mathew, a member of the Award Committee, pointed out. "We are looking for the best examples of these virtues among the 5,000-member strong auto-rickshaw community."

It was on 26 November 2015 that the 32-year-old Noushad, known in his Mavilikkadavu neighborhood as a cheerful and energetic do-gooder, said goodbye to his family and friends as he was suffocated by the toxic fumes emanating from a manhole in a city sewer. While waiting for a mid-morning tea at a wayside cafeteria near Kandankadavu Jubilee Hall in Kozhikode, Noushad heard screams from a manhole. He rushed to the place and saw a Telugu sanitation worker falling unconscious. Another worker had already fallen after inhaling the extremely toxic fumes coming out of the closed sewer. Despite warnings from passers-by, Noushad ventured to lift the two from the sewer but he too fell unconscious and breathed his last. Rescue workers later pulled out the three bodies. Noushad's death was condoled across Kerala and also by the Gulf Malayalees. "The auto drivers in Kozhikode have a legendary reputation across the country for being honest, fair and humane." The then Chief Minister Oommen Chandy announced a cash incentive of Rs.5,00,000/- each to Noushad's mother Asmabi and widow Safreena and a government job for the widow. "Let's hope the award named after Noushad will encourage others to care for human beings and be inspired by his sacrifice," said Mohammed Shaji, Noushad's uncle. Safreena now divides her days between her mother-in-law and her own parents. Noushad now enjoys peace and contentment in his eternal home! (Kozhikode: 27.10.2016)

"The measure of life is not in its duration but in its donation." (P. Marshall)

******

Fr. Shibu Gave Love & Life to Kairunnisa

For Fr. Shibu Yohannan Kuttiparichel (39), Parish Priest at St Mary's Jacobite Church, Cheengeri, in Wayanad, engaging in welfare activities was nothing new. So, when he heard about the health condition of 29-year-old Kairunnisa, hailing from Chavakkad in Thrissur, he decided to donate one of his kidneys. He was inspired by the example of Fr. Davis Chiramel, a Kerala priest who donated a kidney to a stranger five years ago. The harvesting and transplanting of the kidney were done at VPS Lakeshore Hospital, Kochi, in December 2016, under a medical team that included Dr. Abi Abraham, Director of Nephrology and Transplant Services, Dr. George P. Abraham, Transplant Surgeon and Dr. Mohan A. Mathew, Director of Anaesthesiology. "The greatest goodness is to give a helping hand to a falling human being," said Fr. Shibu after giving a heroic example of his love for the suffering humanity, irrespective of caste and creed. The true message of Christmas is: "God gave us his Son, so we are expected to give. So, I just practiced the Christmas message. After becoming a priest, it is the first time I will not be able to celebrate Mass on Christmas day," said Fr. Shibu, who is taking rest in the hospital. It was absolutely a new Christmas experience, a different way of celebrating the birth of the Little One, who came to give abundant life to one and all. This message of Christmas was heard and understood by those around him.

Kairunnisa, the recipient, lives with her bed-ridden husband Shabu, who was paralyzed after a road accident and her three-year-old daughter. Her mother, Shereefa (56), was ready to donate one of her kidneys to her daughter but it was found incompatible. Fr. Shibu chose her as his beneficiary because of her miserable family conditions. Kairunnisa's sister, mother and other relatives came to the hospital to say "Thank You" to Fr. Shibu, but they could not find words to express their feelings of gratitude. Earlier, Fr. Shibu had collected Rs.5,00,000/- and handed it over to the family of Kairunnisa for her husband's medical expenses. The 39-year-old priest has penned several books and uses the money earned from the sale of his works for the treatment of cancer patients. (Manorama, 25.12.2016, Wikipedia)

John's Kidney is Active in a Daily Wager

"When my father passed away in 2011, his eyes were donated. Later when I met the Ophthalmologist who conducted the transplant of my father's eyes on two recipients, he told me how they could see the world again because of my father. That was when I thought of donating my organs," said 45-year-old Sakhi John from Thiruvalla, who is a professor of Management Studies at Jamia Hamdard University in Delhi. "I wanted to give a fresh lease of life to someone while I am alive," he added. So, following his inner call, he donated one of his kidneys to an absolute stranger and a daily wage earner, Shaju Paul (44), who hails from Peechi in Thrissur, whose both kidneys were damaged and was undergoing dialysis. The transplant took place at VPS Lakeshore Hospital, EKM, on 28 December 2016. Shaju was selected as the recipient from among those who had registered with the Kidney Federation of India, founded by Fr. Davis Chiramel, a kidney donor himself.

When Shaju Paul's wife Shibi and children Alwin and Angel were informed that both his kidneys were damaged, they had lost all hope of their beloved father - the sole breadwinner of the family- returning to a normal healthy life. He has undergone 98 dialysis sessions since July 2016. It was then that Sakhi John brought a ray of hope into their lives. John had been working with AIDS patients and was actively associated with an NGO working for slum kids. He met Fr. Chiramel in 2015 and volunteered to donate his kidney. But for the daily wage earner Shaju, the expenses involved in the transplant surgery appeared insurmountable. Then he heard the villagers of Manakkuzhi in Peechi whispering to him: "Why worry, Shaju? We are here to help." They bonded together and collected Rs.22,00,000/- to fund the surgery. A medical team headed by Dr. Abi Abraham, Director, Nephrology & Transplant Services, Dr. George P. Abraham, Transplant Surgeon and Dr. Mohan A. Mathew, Director, Anaesthesiology, performed the harvesting and transplanting of the kidney. (DH, 05.01. 2017).

"The thrill of taking lasts a day. The thrill of giving lasts a lifetime." (B. Carson)

******

Nithin's 20th Birthday Gifts

Nithin did not know to whom he gave and Jenisha did not know from whom she received. Kerala achieved its first ever Heart-Lung Transplantation - an operation where both the heart and the lungs from one person are transplanted to another person - by a team of doctors led by Padmashree Dr. Jose Chacko Periappuram at Lisie Hospital, EKM. Nithin (19), from Karunagappally in Kollam District, was pronounced brain dead following an accident on 04 January 2017. His family, even while shocked by the unexpected and painful departure of Nithin, expressed their willingness to donate his organs. As luck would have it, his organs were found fit to be transplanted to Jenisha (26), daughter of Nirmala and Varghese of Kuttampuzha in EKM, who was diagnosed with Eisenmenger's, which is a rare congenital heart disease. Following the doctor's verdict that only the transplantation of the heart and lungs would ensure her long-term survival, her name was registered under the Mrithasanjeevani program. After a three-hour long surgery, Nithin's organs were simultaneously harvested and transported from Lakeshore Hospital in the city to Lisie Hospital on 06 January 2017, with the help of local police, who set up a green corridor and ensured there was no delay. On the same day, after a seven-hour-long surgery, the transplant was conducted successfully. Four hours after the surgery, the transplanted organs started functioning and in three days' time, Jenisha started breathing on her own. "Jenisha is able to eat, talk and walk. At present, she is kept in the isolation ward to avoid any infection. She can leave the hospital in another week or so if no further complications arise. At the moment, she is hale and hearty," said Dr. Periappuram. Jenisha's family now considers Nidhin as a family member and with folded hands thanks his family. Nithin's pancreas and left kidney were given to a man from Calicut (33) who was under treatment in Amrita Hospital. The liver found a place in a man (61) from Thiruvalla who was being treated at Lakeshore Hospital and his right kidney was given to another patient (56) in the same hospital. Eyes were taken to Little Flower Hospital, Angamaly. On 20 January 2017, Nithin would have celebrated his 20th birthday. (Manorama, 17.01.2017, I.E., 16.01.2017)

"You give little when you give of your possessions. It is when you give of yourself that you truly give." (K. Gibran)

******

Teen's Heart Beats in a Quinquagenarian!

The heart of a 17-year-old boy started beating in a 56-year-old man after a heart transplant was performed in Bengaluru in January 2017. The teen had met with a road accident and was admitted to Fortis Hospital, Bengaluru on 12 January 2017. He was declared brain-dead seven days later. Following his family's consent to organ donation, his heart, liver, kidneys and corneas were harvested. The recipient had suffered heart attacks in 2003 and in 2013, after which he underwent angioplasty but that helped little. His heart's capacity to function reduced progressively and the doctors treating him declared that a heart transplant was the only means for his survival. The teen's heart was sent from Fortis Hospital to Narayana Healthcare, Bengaluru and police created a green corridor at 10.55 pm on Thursday. This helped the ambulance carrying the heart cover a distance of 25 km. in 19 minutes. More details are not available. (DH, 23.01.2017)

"After I die, if my body is donated, I will live to give life and happiness to many." (A. Lincoln)

******

Stem Cells Connected their Hearts

Finally, the donor and the recipient met. Emotionally charged moments for Naval Chaudhary (28), an IT professional from Bengaluru! Grateful, joyful tears flowed freely from Fateh Singh (6) of Amritsar. Naval, the first unrelated bone marrow donor in the country, was able to give a new lease of life to Fateh Singh a year ago. "Till today, I did not know to whom I had donated my bone marrow, but I felt connected to the cute and adorable boy. It is uncommon for the bone marrow of unrelated persons to match. I am happy I could be of help to the little boy," Naval told The Hindu.

Fateh was diagnosed with Thalassemia Major when he was only one-and-a-half years old. During the first blood transfusion, it was discovered that his body was unable to produce antibodies. "He required an urgent blood stem cell transplant," said Sunil Bhat, Paediatric Haemato-Oncologist of Mazumdar Shaw Medical Centre, Bengaluru, who had conducted the bone marrow transplant in 2016. Naval had registered with the DATRI (Donor in Sanskrit) Blood Stem Cell Donors Registry in 2015 at a camp held in his workplace. Within a year of his registration, he received a call from DATRI informing him that he was a perfect match for a six-year-old suffering from an acute form of thalassemia who required an urgent blood stem cell transplant. "We see a number of patients suffering from fatal blood disorders like blood cancer and thalassemia, for which the last resort is cell transplant. For many years there was no hope for such patients. But registries like DATRI are changing the situation," said Dr. Bhat, who conducted the transplant. As per the registry protocol, the identity of the donors and the recipients is kept anonymous for one year. The parents of Fateh Singh searched for words to verbalize their gratitude to   Naval. "You are our savior and a part of our family now," said Neeta Singh, the boy's mother. (The Hindu, 09.03.2017)

"Be an organ donor; all it costs is a little love."
******

Surendran is Merry because of Merin

Sr. Merin Paul's name has been written in gold in Heaven's Book of Life as Merin Paul, the Saviour of Surendran Shaju. A well-deserved accolade, indeed! Sr. Merin, HM of Infant Jesus High School, Aranattukara, Thrissur, on her retirement, took the resolution to donate one of her kidneys to a needy person. When she heard of Surendran's (37) case, she decided to give flesh and blood to her resolve. Surendran's family consists of his mother, wife and two siblings. He was an employee in a company that prepares cushions of varied shapes, colors and materials and the modest income he procured was the only means he had to satiate five hungry bellies and to meet other household expenses. A rare sickness affected his kidneys 16 years ago at the age of 21 and his right kidney had stopped functioning and had been removed. Now at the age of 37, the only surviving kidney too became dysfunctional. Five years ago, he registered his name in the Kidney Federation of India in search of a suitable kidney. After the required tests, Sr. Merin's kidney was found fit and the transplant was done in April 2017, at VPS Lakeshore Hospital, Kochi, by an expert team of doctors consisting of George P. Abraham, Datson George, Vijay Radhakrishnan (Urology), Mohan Mathew (Anaesthesia), and Aby Abraham (Nephrologist). Now, Merin's kidney smiles in gratitude from Surendran's body. "I did not donate my kidney for money or publicity. I have been looking forward to saving a life through a personal sacrifice," said Sr. Merin Paul. *Dear Sr. Merin Paul, may you continue to be a blessing to your fellow humans!* (Manorama, 06.04.2017)

"You don't have to be a doctor to save lives.
You can save lives by donating your organs."
******

Crispin, the Christ Bearer

"To save my mother's life, share this post." This was the desperate cry, via Facebook post, of Christin Varghese, the son of a financially low-income family in Pulinkunnu, Alappuzha. The post was in search of anyone who was willing to donate a kidney to his mother, Philomena, who was under treatment due to a malfunctioning kidney. Christin did not have much hope of a positive response from anyone. Out of love for his mother, he just tried his luck. But it was heard by Fr. Crispin John (35) in faraway Himachal Pradesh. Moved by his passion for Christ and compassion for humanity, after making sure that the need was genuine, without wasting time, with the blessings of his parents and co-friars, Fr. Crispin, the son of John and Philomena of Kovilthottam, Kollam, resolved to give flesh and blood to the command of his God: "Love one another as I have loved you" and decided to help the struggling family in need. He traveled from H.P. and presented himself at Pushpagiri Medical College Hospital, Thiruvalla. All the tests proved him to be a fitting donor and the recipient too responded positively. After the transplant, Crispin might have whispered in his heart: Done! For Christ and for His poor! Thus, Philomena's son Crispin donated his kidney to another Philomena, the mother of Christin. A happy coincidence of names!

Fr. Crispin, who was working in Delhi, was transferred to H.P. only recently. The call for help from a poor family on behalf of the suffering mother came when he was busy with his teaching and evangelization ministries. He wanted very much to keep it a secret but Rev. Fr. John Baptist of Pentecostal Church thought differently and decided that those who look only for their own comforts should know this act of generosity and Manorama took it up. (Manorama, 09.05.2017)

"You have two kidneys but you need only one. The power of the extra one is that it can allow someone to live a whole new life." (H. Gerrits)

******

Atul-Bhatt Heart Rendezvous

Subramanyam Bhatt (50), who had been struggling due to heart ailments, received a new lease on life and as he slowly springs back to life, many persons are on his Thank You list but the first name written in gold is that of Atulkumar Pawar (24) a sub-lieutenant of Dronacharya, Kochi. Atulkumar, the son of Rajbir Singh Pawar from Panchkula, Haryana, was returning from Wayanad after a picnic with his friends when the group met with an accident and Atul was severely injured. He was taken to Aster Medicity, Kochi, where the combined efforts of a team of doctors and nurses proved futile and he was declared brain dead. The grief-stricken parents proved their mettle and expressed their wish to donate their son's organs to someone serving in the Navy. The procedures to harvest his organs began immediately with the National Organ & Tissue Transplant Organization (NOTTO) which is a project of the Union Govt. for the post-death transplant of organs was contacted. At around 10.00 pm on Wednesday 27 September 2017, Medical College Hospital (MCH), Kottayam, received the news of the availability of a healthy young heart fit for transplantation. Immediately, Subramanyam Bhatt, a native of EKM who had been waiting for a matching heart for over a year after registering his name in an organ donation project, was admitted to the hospital. At 07.00 am on 28 September 2017, a team of doctors from MCH, Kottayam, left for Kochi and carrying the precious cargo reached back to MCH by 11 am. The heart of young Atul was successfully transplanted onto the body of Bhatt after a long, complex surgery led by Dr. Jayakumar, the Head of the Cardiology Dept. of MCH. By 03.30 pm, Atul's heart started beating gratefully in Bhatt's body. While Bhatt was lying unconscious on the operation table, his partially blind wife Maya and his two daughters Bhavyasree and Sasikala were standing outside, with their hearts and hands lifted up to heaven. Though Atulkumar, the young naval officer, lost his life, he left this world as a good humanitarian, giving life to others. His one kidney flew to Command Hospital, Bengaluru; meanwhile, his second kidney and liver were taken to Aster Medicity, Kochi.

Giving a ray of hope to thousands of patients, the first heart transplant surgery in a Government Medical College in the State was done in MCH, Kottayam, in September 2015, with Atul-Bhatt-Heart rendezvous being the fourth transplant. (Deepika, 19.09.2017, website)

"Don't take your organs to heaven.
Heaven knows we need them here."
******

Shreya Works with Sachin's Hands

Shreya (19), the only daughter of Suma Nuggihalli and Fakirgowda Siddnagowda from Pune, lost both her hands in a bus accident while she was traveling from Pune to Mangaluru in September 2016. She was rushed to the hospital, where both her arms were amputated at the elbow. Sachin, the son of K.S. Radhakrishnan Nair and Baby Girija, a

20-year-old B. Com final year student of Rajagiri College, Kochi, was declared brain dead on 09 September 2017, after he suffered a fatal head injury in a motorcycle accident. His grief-stricken parents, though wriggling under the pain of loss, agreed to donate his hands and other organs.

Dr K. Subramania Iyer, Head of the Department of Head & Neck Surgery, Amrita School of Medical Sciences, Kochi, led a 36-member team of doctors, including 20 surgeons, for the transplant of Sachin's hands into Shreya's body. After 13-hour-long inter-gender double hand surgery, the first of its kind in Asia, Maharashtrian Shreya left the surgery table with Malayali Sachin's hands. Later, the hospital authorities confirmed that Sachin's hands have adapted to the new situation and the recipient is able to move her hands and in two years' time, the hands will regain about 80% mobility. Shreya, who is a Chemical Engineering student at the Institute of Technology, Manipal, said that the hands of the male donor Sachin had lost some of their weight and her new hands looked like a natural fit to her and expressed her heartfelt gratitude to Sachin's parents. (Deepika 28.09.2017

*"The meaning of life is to find your gift.
The purpose of life is to give it away."* (P. Picasso)
*****

Rose, a Rare Fragrant Flower

On the occasion of the Silver Jubilee of her religious profession, Dr Sr. Rose Anto, HoD of the Hindi Dept., St. Joseph's College, Irinjalakuda, Thrissur, gifted one of her kidneys to Thilakan of Azad Road, Irinjalakuda. Thilakan (47), the father of two kids, was struggling to make ends meet from his meager income from repairing cycles and doing other odd jobs. He was diagnosed with chronic renal ailments, which resulted in the failure of both kidneys. Dialysis and medications followed. Finally, the heart-breaking verdict of the doctors! "Thilakan's malfunctioning kidneys are beyond repair or rejuvenation; kidney transplant is the only solution." Hearing of the pathetic predicament of Thilakan, his neighbors and well-wishers formed a committee to create awareness of his painful condition and to raise funds for the medical expenses involved in the transplant. Humanitarian Rose Anto, who is widely known and much loved in and around Irinjalakuda, who regularly offers support and sustenance to the elderly and poor widows, did not have to think twice before she stepped forward and said: "Here I am" and agreed to donate one of her kidneys. After the necessary tests, on 19 January 2017, the transplant was conducted by a medical team led by Dr George P. Abraham at VPS Lakeshore Hospital, Kochi and Rose's kidney started its service to Thilakan's body. A special jubilee celebration indeed!

"Sister was sent by God as an angel to save my life," said Thilakan. His wife Saritha said: "Without Sr. Rose's kindness, my husband wouldn't have been alive today. We are deeply indebted to her." "God gave me an opportunity to donate my kidney, in the jubilee year of my religious life, to a person who needed it most," said Sr. Rose, who hails from Kaithavana, Alappuzha and is one of 12 siblings. She is widely hailed and appreciated for her unique project - Penn Marangal (Girl trees) - of planting a tree at the birth of a girl child anywhere in the Irinjalakuda constituency. *Dear Rose Anto, you are true to your name; you spread the fragrance of rose with your other-centered life!* (Deepika, 06.10.2017; Wikipedia)

"You were born with the ability to change someone's life. Don't waste it."

******

Wilson & Abhirami are Life-Partners

While watching a TV channel, Wilson heard about the two-and-a-half-year-old Abhirami (Abhi) who was born with a malfunctioning liver. Instantly, his innate sense of compassion flowed freely from his humane heart. Wilson Varghese (29) of Konni, Pathanamthitta, did not tarry long, before deciding to share his fully functioning liver with the little one. His wife Annie and daughter Little Therese stood firmly by his side, with fervent prayers in their hearts. Just four days after her birth, Abhi, the only child of Anilkumar and Renu of Alappuzha, was affected by jaundice (Hepatitis B) which was followed by serious liver problems. A hard solution came from the medical world. A donor has to be found and a transplant surgery should follow, which would cost nothing less than Rs.20,00,000/- As soon as Wilson communicated his willingness to donate part of his liver, Abhi's grateful family heaved a sigh of relief and Aster Medicity, Kochi started preparations for the transplant. Deepika reported on 03 August 2018: "Today at Aster Medicity, Kochi, Wilson, the donor and Abhirami, the receiver, will undergo the transplant surgery." Wilson is a member of St. Mary's Malankara Catholic Church and the Parish Priest, Fr. Daniel Kozhuvakatt, certified that Wilson is a very active member of the parish.

NB. In a liver transplant surgery, a portion of the liver from a healthy living person is removed and placed into the recipient whose liver is non-functional. The donor's remaining liver regrows and gains its normal size, volume and capacity within a couple of months after the surgery. In the same way, the transplanted liver portion grows and becomes a healthy and functioning liver in the recipient.

*"Organ donation is not a tragedy.
It is a beautiful light in the midst of a tragedy."*
****

Mary Salin is Salt and Life

"Love your neighbor as yourself" is the command of Jesus. But Mary Salin (50), a member of Mary Immaculate Church, Marygiri, Malayatoor, EKM, loved her neighbor more than herself and donated one of her kidneys to Rosmi (23), her neighbor. Mary is a teacher at Anitha English Medium School, Thannipuzha, EKM. For the last 10 years, she has been associated with Sunday School in her parish and also serves as the Area Council Secretary of Vincent de Paul Society, a social service organization. Salin's neighbor Rosmi, a nurse, has been suffering from kidney problems even from her student days. Rosmi's father, Joy Pallicka, a daily wager, finds it difficult to make ends meet. After spending whatever they could afford for Rosmi's treatment, the family was told that a kidney transplant alone would put her on her feet. Hearing about the predicament of Rosmi, our heroine Mary Salin, a widow and the mother of two sons, decided to lend a helping hand to her suffering, struggling neighbor and volunteered to donate one kidney. The parishioners, under the leadership of Fr. Joshy Kalaparampath, had a collection drive to raise the money needed to meet the hospital expenses. While the transplant surgery was progressing in the hospital, the parishioners gathered in their church to pray for the success of the transplant and Rosmi's speedy recovery. How could a merciful God not hear their earnest prayers when kindness and compassion flowed so freely from His children? (Deepika, 23.10.2018)

"Do you want to live on after you are gone?
Take a simple step, donate your organs."
******

Ajay Lived Up to His Name

Ajay means unconquerable! The hero of this episode, Ajay, the only son of the Johny-Shirley couple hailing from Cheranallor, EKM, lived up to his name. Johny, a day laborer together with his wife had entertained dreams about Ajay, that after his studies, he would find a decent job and a loving life partner and live a relaxed, contented life. All these wishes and dreams were crushed on the Varappuzha overbridge, where Ajay met with an accident and was seriously hurt. He was admitted to Aster Medicity, Kochi but all the efforts of the medical fraternity to get him back on his feet failed. Ajay's dream of providing a restful life to his parents died when on 05 March 2019, at the age of 19, Ajay flew from his earthly abode to his Forever Home. Though Ajay was temporarily conquered by death, his parents refused to bow before death or say goodbye to their son. Unconquered by death, now Ajay lives in four other humans unknown to him but very much known and loved by his parents. Under the leadership of Dr Mathew Jacob, Multi-Organ Transplant Surgeon of Aster Medicity, Ajay's liver was transplanted to a patient in the same hospital. One kidney and pancreas now function in two patients who were then under treatment at Amritha Hospital, Kochi. The second kidney is active in a person who was then being treated for a damaged kidney in Medical College Hospital, Kozhikode. So, Ajay, the winner, lives on in four different persons in four different homes. (Deepika, 06.03.2019)

(A. Lincoln)
******

Anujith Gave Life to Many

Some lives make the world around them beautiful, even in the face of death. Anujith was a teenager when he ran with his friends across a railway track in Kerala, frantically trying to warn an approaching train against a crack in the track. Their signaling worked. An accident was avoided and hundreds of lives were saved thanks to the foresightedness of Anujith, then an ITI student in Kottarakkara. Newspapers and social media celebrated Anujith and his friends for their bravery and timely action.

That was 10 years ago, in August 2010. In July 2020, Anujith was in the news again for another commendable act, but he was no longer around to read the news item. Anujith, who was employed as a driver with a private company, lost his job due to the lockdown and was working as a salesman in a supermarket in Kottarakkara. He died in an accident on 14 July 2020 while he was riding a bike near Kottarakkara, but not before pledging his organs to those in need. While undergoing treatment at the KIMS Hospital in TVPM, the doctors declared him brain dead. His wife, Princy, was aware of his wish to donate his organs in case of death. The News Minute quoted the bereaved wife. "This is what he last told me - that if he is not there in the world anymore, let someone else live through him. It was his last wish and we are going ahead to fulfill his wish. He helped many people while he was alive and now, even in his death, he is helping others." His heart was flown from KIMS Hospital in TVPM to Lisie Hospital in Kochi, where 55-year-old Sunny Joseph, a native of Thripunithura, woke up to life and love on the operating table with Anujith's heart beating gratefully in his body. Thanks to Anujith's benevolent heart, his kidneys, eyes, small intestine and hands were donated so that they could be used by others in need Google gives the meaning of Anujit as a born leader, thinker, focused and dedicated.(The Hindu, Manorama & Deepika, 22.07. 2020)

"Since we cannot take our organs to the afterlife,
the best thing to do is to donate them."

******

Arvind Gifted, Surya Received

Lotus blossoms after the sun rises from its night rest. In the following event, Surya (sun) rose from his sick bed with a smile because Arvind (lotus) gave up his life. Suryanarayanan (18) from Kayamkulam, Alappuzha, was suffering from a disease known as Dilated Cardio-Mayopathi which causes undue enlargement of the heart. Almost on the point of slipping into eternity, he was admitted to Lisie Hospital, Kochi and gave his life into the hands of the internationally famous Dr. Chacko Periappuram and his expert team. Detailed and elaborate tests and examinations followed. The final verdict was unequivocal: "If the present state of his heart continues, Surya will say goodbye to his earthly sojourn within a few days. Hence, a heart transplant is the only solution."

As the parents of Surya threw up their hands in despair, wondering what to do next, they heaved a sigh of relief at the much-awaited hopeful news from Kerala Institute of Medical Sciences (KIMS) Hospital, TVPM. Three days after Surya was admitted to Lisie Hospital, Dr. Noble Gracious, Nodal Officer of Kerala Network for Organ Sharing, communicated the news that a heart was available. The beating, pulsating heart of Arvind (25), who died of an accident at Nagercoil, flew across the sky in a helicopter and reached Kochi. Tests and re-tests! Heads, hearts and hands worked in harmony to transfer the heart of Arvind to Surya's body. Then the final hope-filled message! Arvind's heart will beat in Surya's body! A few days later, Surya and his parents left the hospital, thanking the doctors and praying for Arvind's parents and siblings. (Manorama & Deepika, 08.03.2021)

"There is nothing better than being able to give
a healthy organ to improve the life of another person."
******

Nevis' Heart Beats in Premchand's

The ambulance carrying a precious gift of life left Kochi at around 04.15 pm on 25 September 2021 and reached Metromed International Cardiac Centre, Kozhikode, at 07.15 pm. A five-hour-long surgery to transplant the heart of Nevis (25) of Kottayam to Premchand (59) of Kannur began immediately under the expert guidance of Dr V. Nandakumar, helped by a team of doctors and nurses. On the following day, by 03 am, Nevis' heart started to sing the song of life and love in Premchand's body.

Nevis did his schooling at Girideepam Bethany Central School, Kottayam. His teacher Annammal Abraham testifies that he was good in studies and music while in school. He was pursuing his post-graduate studies in France, had returned home in the wake of COVID-19 and was planning to go back to France on 29 September 2021. On the morning of 16 September 2019, his family members found him unconscious in bed. He was rushed to Caritas Hospital, Kottayam and later was shifted to Rajagiri Hospital, Aluva, EKM, for better treatment and care. Three days ahead of World Heart Day, he was declared brain dead. The grief-stricken parents of Nevis - Sajan Mathew and Sherine - found a very humanitarian way to overcome their sorrow by helping others in distress. His heart, kidneys, hands, liver and corneas were donated to different patients under the State Govt.'s Mritha-sanjeevani, Kerala Network for Organ Sharing. Now Nevis' parents find comfort in the fact that their son, though not with them, lives on in many other sons and daughters. His mortal remains were interred in St. Thomas Malankara Catholic Church Cemetery, Sasthri Road, Kalathipadi, Kottayam, on 28 September 2021. May Nevis rest in peace in his eternal home above! (The Hindu, Mathrubhoomi & Manorama dated respectively 26, 27 & 28.09.2021)

"We make a living by what we get. We make a life by what we give." (W. Churchill)
******

Death to Albin Paul, Life to Six Others

Albin Paul, a 30-year-old native of Thrissur who flew to his eternal home beyond the clouds in October 2021, will continue to live through six people who received six of his organs. The organ transplant extended as far as Chennai since a matching recipient for Albins' heart could not be found in Kerala. According to the release issued by the Office of the Minister for Health, Women and Child Development, Albin and his brother Sebin had gone to Cochin International Airport to see off a relative. On their way back, their car collided with a lorry at 3.15 am on 18 October 2021 and both suffered grave injuries and were admitted at Apollo Adlux Hospital, Angamaly, EKM. His brother Sebin recovered and left the hospital. After Albin was declared brain dead, his father Paulose consented to organ donation. His heart, liver, kidneys and eyes were harvested for donation through the govt.'s Mritha-sanjeevani program coordinated by the Kerala Network for Organ Sharing (KNOS). In the absence of a matching heart recipient registered under the Mritha-sanjeevani, the same was reported to the National Organ and Tissue Transplantation Organisation (NOTTO) that shared the details of the case with the Regional Organ and Tissue Transplantation Organisation (ROTTO). Soon, a recipient was identified at Rela Hospital in

Chennai. A kidney was allocated for a patient who was being treated at Govt. Medical College Hospital, TVPM. Albin is survived by his wife, a four-month-old baby, parents and brother. (25.10. 2021, TVPM)

"There is no bigger donation than donating your organs."
******

Narayan Embraced Death to Save Another

Narayan literally means eternal man. Now Narayan Dabhalkar lives eternally with his God. "There is no greater love than this that a person would lay down his life for the sake of his friends." Not sure whether 85-year-old Narayan Dabhalkar, a resident of Savithri Nagar, Nagpur, had heard/read this biblical statement. Even if he did not have the theoretical knowledge of the statement above, he showed how to translate it into a real-life situation. What is more? He gave his life not for a friend but for an absolute stranger! While receiving the necessary attention from the doctors and nurses in the hospital, Narayan noticed the wife of a young man knocking at many doors in search of a hospital bed for her husband (40), who too was affected by the rogue virus. Knowing the urgency of the need of the moment, Narayan expressed his readiness to be discharged from the hospital and thus vacate the bed to accommodate the young man whose need was more urgent than his own. "I have lived my life; now I want to save the life of this young man. He must live for the sake of his small children. So, I want to give my bed to him," said the octogenarian Narayan, who was admitted to the hospital on 22 April 2021 following the attack of the killer virus, which resulted in the deficient intake of oxygen. His family members and doctors objected to the idea. But our other-centered hero was determined and repeated: "Please, allow me to give my bed to that young man." Righto! Golden-hearted Narayan returned home and on the following day, he said goodbye to his earthly home, leaving behind the aroma of a life spent for the benefit of another. "To bring a young man back to life, the good man Narayan Dabhalkar gave his life," said Dr Ajay Haridas of Indira Gandhi Hospital, Nagpur. *Our grateful salute to you, good-hearted Grandpa Narayan!*

> **"Learn to light a candle in the darkest moments of someone's life. It is what gives life its deepest significance."**
> (Roy T. Bennett)

******

Baby Nirvan is on the Way to Nirvana

In January 2023, Nirvan, the 15-month-old son of Sarang Menon and Adithi Nair, was diagnosed with Spinal Muscular Atrophy (SMA), a rare genetic disease that causes muscle weakness and progressive loss of movement due to the deterioration of motor neurons. The disease makes breathing and intake of food difficult and if left untreated, it can lead to permanent ventilation or death. Treatment for SMA costs about Rs. 17.5 crore and the drug known as Zolgensma is one of the world's most expensive drugs marketed by Novartis, a global healthcare company based in Switzerland. It is a one-time drug for the disease, which is currently not available in India, but can be imported from the USA with a medical prescription and a letter from the guardian of the child to the company.

Nirvan's parents had started crowdfunding a few weeks earlier and till 19 February 2023, they had collected Rs.5.42 crore. On 20 February the family announced on their Facebook page: "We are grateful to you all for your unwavering support, prayers and contributions towards Nirvaan's SMA treatment. Your compassion and kindness towards our family have given us the strength to keep fighting along with our son's fight against SMA. We want to share a piece of good news with you all - we have received a significant donation of

$1.4 million from an anonymous donor. Their generosity has brought us closer to our goal of raising funds needed for Nirvan's treatment. It is heart-warming to know that there are still angels of charity in the world who selflessly come forward to help others in need. I urge you all to continue praying for his fast recovery, as he still has a long road ahead. But for now, let's take a moment to celebrate this wonderful news and the kindness of the donor who has made it possible. We do not know who donated the money. It is like a miracle for us. I usually check Milaap (crowdfunding platform) at least 10 times a day to see if there's any contribution. And yesterday, there was a sudden jump in donations. When I contacted Milaap about it, they said it was made by a single individual. The person did not want to reveal his/her identity," Nirvan's father, Sarang Menon, told TNM. "I came to know of the child's plight through the media; I felt I should chip in. I'm donating the money, not for fame. Even the child's parents should not know my name. The life of the child is important, not my name," the unknown Good Samaritan told the crowdfunding agency. The touching gesture has brought fresh hope to the parents and doctors. The US pharmaceutical company officials assured that the medicine will be sent shortly to the doctors in Mumbai. Nirvaan's father, Sarang, is a Merchant

Navy employee and his mother, Adithi Nair, is a software engineer. They hail from Malalath House, Koottanadu, Palakkad. The family hopes to collect the remaining money by the time the bill is to be settled. (Mathrubhoomi & Manorama, 22.02.2022)

"Let not your left hand know what your right hand is doing." (Bible)

******

New Life to Rajalal via Priyanka

S.S. Rajalal, CPM Area Secretary of Peroorkada, TVPM, was in the hospital fighting an unrelenting battle against his non-cooperative, non-functioning liver. Priyanka (29), the Joint Secretary of DYFI, Karakulam and an employee of Service Co-operative Bank, was aware that Rajalal was sick, but she came to know of the need to replace his malfunctioning liver through a party member Prashanth. Without much thought and discussion with friends or party workers, Priyanka decided to part with a bit of her liver in favor of Rajalal, who is a much loved and sought-after party worker and actively involved in the life of the people of the area. Priyanka told her friends that her decision was not based on any outside influence and requested that her name as the donor should not be revealed till the surgery was over. She underwent surgery, which lasted for

12 hours, in Aster Medicity, Kochi, on 12 July 2022. Her days in the ICU after the surgery were days of unspeakable pain and discomfort, including her distress in not being able to see her daughter Theerdha who was being cared for by Ajana, her friend. The world around her came to know of her heroic generosity through her Facebook post after she left the hospital; she posted: "Organ donation is a great thing one can do while alive, a great good deed to save the life of another!" Both the donor and the receiver are getting ready to go back to normal life after their hospital stay and rest. (Manorama, 20.08.2022)

"Give yourself and those in need an elixir of life by pledging your organs." (Mohith Agadi)

******

Brave Man Dheeraj with a Giving Heart

Dheeraj (meaning brave) 44, resident of Kattoor, Thrissur, leaving behind his wife Jifna, his children Kripa Maria, Chrismario, Christiano and Charismaria and brother Sooraj, took his flight to the ever-green land beyond the clouds and presented himself to the Lord of heaven on 13 December 2022. Though he is no more on earth with his family and friends, he lives on in four others of God's children. Earlier in December 2022, he was admitted to a private hospital in Thrissur due to severe headache and vomiting and was diagnosed with excessive bleeding in the brain. Soon he was shifted to a private hospital in Kochi. After the surgery, his condition worsened and he was transferred to Aster Medcity, Kochi. At 07.15 pm on 13 December 2022, he was declared brain dead. Though grief-stricken, Dheeraj's family remembered his often-expressed wish to donate his organs if and when death came to claim him. Dheeraj's liver was transplanted into a 46-year-old man from Puthenchira, Thrissur, who was being treated at Aster Medcity. One of his kidneys was given to Government Medical College, Kottayam and the other to the Medical Trust Hospital, Kochi. Both corneas were donated to Giridhar Eye Hospital, Kochi. Bravo! Dheeraj defeated death and lives on! (Manorama, Kochi edition, 16.12.2022)

"What we are doing is nothing more than a drop in the ocean. If that drop were not there, the ocean would be missing something." (Mother Teresa)

Bella Manoj - Kidney Donor, Solo Rider

"There are some places in life where you must go alone. Embrace the beauty of the solo journey." Bella Manoj, the passionate solo rider who lives with her husband Manoj and her daughter Ivy in Chennai, is translating the above quote into her life. But before we travel along with her, here is her story.

"I want to prove that a person can live a normal life with one kidney. My husband almost died of kidney failure; then, I decided, despite his objections, to donate one of my kidneys. I am totally healthy and fine after the surgery. Unfortunately, many kidney patients in our country die unable to find a donor. I am sharing my story to inspire others in similar situations," said Bella. When she fell in love with solo travel earlier this year, she decided to use it as a means to prove a point. Six years after donating one of her kidneys to Manoj Matthan her husband, Bella is on a cross-country motorcycle ride, albeit in stages, to experience the thrill of exploring places and spreading the word about the importance of kidney donation. "Nothing beats the joy of traveling alone and exploring new places," says the 50-year-old fashion designer who is currently on the final leg of a tour of Tamil Nadu and Kerala. In the two trips she made on her Royal

Enfield Bullet 500 in the past six months, she has traveled over 12,500 km, covering 13 Indian States and five Union Territories. "I have been riding a motorcycle for several years. But never went beyond a certain distance until I rode my bullet to Velankanni in March of this year. Later I made a trip to Bengaluru and I immediately realized I have to do more of this," says Bella from Punnapra, Alappuzha. In June 2022, she went on a road trip from Chennai, riding along the West Coast to Rajasthan, Punjab, Jammu and Kashmir and all the way to Ladakh. "It was a 30-day trip. After reaching Ladakh, I spent a week there exploring places such as Kargil, Leh, Khardung La, Hunder, Pangong Tso, Kharoo and Sarchu. On my return journey, I traveled through North and Central India. Traveling solo is extremely challenging but it is fun too, to be nobody but you," says Bella, a graduate of the National Institute of Fashion Technology. She is planning her next trip to Northeast India. She has also pledged to donate her body to medical science after her death. *Bella, (means beautiful) you are a beautiful person in your thoughts and deeds!* (The Hindu, 31.12.2022)

"Be a Thinker, Be a Doer, Be a Donor."

******

Celine Walked the Talk

As a motivational speaker, Organ Challenge was the pet theme of Celine Christopher (62), Kochikkaran Veedu, Chettikadu, Alappuzha. Her oft-repeated slogan was, "Don't take your organs to heaven; we need them here." As a palliative care nurse, she has motivated many older and younger generations about the need and meaning of organ donation and has conducted awareness classes for many years along the coastal townships and villages of Alappuzha, explaining the need and relevance of organ donation. True to her convictions and teaching, almost 20 years prior to her final goodbye to Mother Earth, Celine had written her Will, expressing her decision to donate her eyes after her death. While she was under treatment at the ESI Hospital, Alappuzha, for certain cardiac problems, on 01 February 2023, Celine said goodbye to her munificent activities and flew to the bosom of her Father in heaven. After being informed about her demise, doctors from Medical College Hospital Alappuzha reached her house and harvested her corneas. Celine will continue to see her loved ones and enjoy the sight of dancing flowers, singing birds, moving clouds, setting sun, pouring rain and more through the eyes of two co-humans. Inspired by her motivational sessions, her neighbor Anchuthaickal Kathreena's eyes were donated after her death. Following Celine's example, her husband Christopher, children Clint, Christy and Shalini, daughter-in-law Simi and son-in-law Kannan have signed their Will to donate their eyes after their final goodbyes. (Mathrubhoomi, 03.02.2023)

Eyes: Useless to the Dead!
Priceless to the Blind!
******

Shyamala & Rajesh Now Blood Relatives

M.R. Rajesh (35), a native of Payipad, Changanassery, had been suffering from serious heart ailments for the last four years and was being treated at Govt. Medical College Hospital, Kottayam. About a year ago, he registered his name with the Mritha-Sanjeevani project of the Govt. of Kerala. When Shyamala Ramakrishnan (52), a native of Hyderabad who was under treatment at Aster Medicity, Kochi, was declared brain dead, Shyamala's son Subramanyan expressed his willingness to donate the organs of his mother. After the necessary tests, the medical team found Shyamala a fitting donor and Rajesh as a needy recipient. A team of doctors, under the leadership of Dr. T.K. Jayakumar, left Aster Medicity at 11.45 am on 25 March 2023 with the pulsating heart of Shyamala and reached MCH, Kottayam at 12.47 pm. After the transplant surgery, which lasted two and a half hours, Rajesh was shifted to the Intensive Care Unit (ICU) of the hospital. Now Shyamala's heart beats rhythmically, gratefully in Rajesh's body! Shyamala's life ended - no, not correct - Shyamala continues to live as she gave new life to six people by donating her heart, liver, two kidneys and two eyes. Health Minister Veena George congratulated Dr. Jayakumar and the team and thanked the family members of Shyamala who thought of others in distress even while their own hearts were bleeding with sorrow. This was the eighth heart transplant surgery at MCH, Kottayam. (Manorama, 26.03.3023)

"Recycle yourself; be an organ donor."
******

Death Died, Sarangh Lives On

Sarangh closed his eyes temporarily in death on 17 May 2023. They opened again in the body of two co-humans deprived of eyesight. B.R. Sarangh, (16) a student of Std. X, Boy's School, Attingal, TVPM, son of Binish Kumar and Rajani, Nadackaparambil House, Vanchiyoor, was traveling in an auto together with his mother on 06 May 2023 when he met with an accident. As 4,19,128 students, their teachers and parents, together with the whole of Kerala, were waiting with bated breath for the announcement of the SSLC Exam 2023 result, Sarangh's parents waited with agonizing breath for a hope-filled word from the doctors. Instead, what they heard was the heartbreaking news of his brain death. When Minister V. Sivankutty officially declared the SSLC results on 20 May 2023, Sarangh's dear ones, teachers and friends were giving Sarangh, who passed SSLC with full A+, their teary-eyed, final salute. Before saluting the SSLC exam winners, the whole of Kerala bowed in awe and respect to the parents of Sarangh, who agreed to donate his organs. His heart was immediately taken to Kottayam and it will continue to throb gratefully in the heart of a young boy. His eyes, hands, liver and kidneys were donated. Let's bow in thanks to Binish Kumar and Rajani, the generous parents of Sarangh who, even while drowning in an ocean of sorrow, thought of others and did what they could to bring cheer to a few. (Manorama,18 & 19. 05. 2023, Mathrubhoomi 20.05.2023)

"When there is an organ donor, life springs from death, sorrow turns into hope and a terrible loss becomes a gift."
******

Fr. James' Kidney Sings in Jojo's Body

Jojo of Nedumbasserry, a Hotel Manager at Angamaly, has been suffering from malfunctioning kidneys for a long time and had registered his name with the Mritha-Sanjivani, a project of the government to help patients who need organ transplants. After spending much money and time on treatment, the verdict came from the medical fraternity that the only way for Jojo to continue to occupy his given space on this planet was a kidney transplant. Fr. James Kunthara, CMI, heard about Jojo's problem through Bro. Thomas, a relative of Jojo, doing his priestly studies at Pope John Paul II's Seminary, Neeleswaram. Immediately through Thomas, Fr. James conveyed his readiness to donate one of his healthy kidneys to Jojo. The good news flew fast and sure to Jojo's family. On 17 May 2023, a medical team consisting of specialist doctors of Rajagiri Hospital, Aluva - Dr. Jose Thomas, Dr. Balagopal Nair, Dr. Sneha P. Simon, Dr. Appu

Jose, Dr. Sachin George, Dr. Shalini Ramakrishanan - conducted the transplant successfully. In the first week of June 2023, Jojo left the hospital with a vital part of Fr. James' body functioning gratefully in his body. *Three cheers - nay - three million cheers to Fr. James CMI! May your tribe increase!!* (Deepika, 08.06.2023)

"I am only one, but still I am one.
I cannot do everything,
but still I can do something,
And because I cannot do everything
I will not refuse to do something I can do."
(E. E. Hale)

PART 2: THEY WAGERED THEIR LIVES

Rescuers Kannan-Vineetha Duo

A congratulatory meeting is on at St. Aloysius High School, Edathua, Alappuzha. Kannan, the hero of the day, is being carried on the shoulders of his classmates with loud-throated singing and frenetic dancing. But what is the reason for this unusual merriment? Here it is! As Kannan was walking along a river, he heard the desperate cry of little Adarsh of Std. II, who was almost drowning. Without waiting to calculate his ability to swim or carry the little one on his shoulders to safety, Kannan jumped into the river and moved a little towards the river bank. But when he realized he couldn't move forward anymore, he cried aloud and called for help. Vineetha Sinu, an L.P School teacher who momentarily forgot her back pain and other ailments, pulled the victim and the savior to safety. The above celebration was part of the program Fr. John Manakunnel, the Manager and the PTA of the school together organized to congratulate the courageous saviors - student Kannan and Teacher Vineetha. With tears of joy and gratitude flowing freely, Adarsh's father, Shaji, was part of the celebration. Edathua Panchayat is planning another congratulatory meeting to propose Kannan's name for the President's Award for Bravery. (Deepika 23.08.2017)

Ambulance Koottayma's Mission

"I am sad, very sad! Death claimed him! We were not able to save this tiny life!" These are the regretful words of Shajuddin Chirackal, who piloted the Ambulance *Koottayma* (fellowship), which was on its wingless flight to reach TVPM on 05 October 2017 to save the life of two-and-half-month-old Mohammed Hanan, the son of Shoukath Ali and Salmath. Hanan was born with a malfunctioning heart and was undergoing treatment in Dhanalakshmi Hospital, Kannur. As the tiny tot's condition worsened, doctors suggested that the little one be taken to Sri Chithira Hospital, TVPM, for better treatment.

It was only three months earlier that an Ambulance WhatsApp group was formed in the State with Shajuddin as its coordinator. Within this short time, they have helped 17 little angels (including a one-day-old new-born with whom they literally flew from Kozhikode to Vellore in Tamil Nadu) who were almost at death's door and were in need of better treatment by taking them to different hospitals on time. The desperately urgent call to take Hanan from Kannur to Sri Chithira Hospital, TVPM, reached the WhatsApp group after 06.00 pm on 04 October 2017. The ambulance reached Kannur at 5.10 am on the following day and started its journey back at break-neck speed along the highway by 07.10 am. A convoy of 12 pilot ambulances sped ahead to clear the road. On busy streets, the people of the area lent the needed helping hand. Medical reports and other necessary information had already been sent to the hospital. Shajuddin Chirackal, Sulfi Chavakad and others had already calculated the time when they would reach TVPM. The message from Sri Chithira at 03.00 pm, which said that the team of doctors was ready and waiting for the angelic patient to perform emergency surgery, gave faster wings to their flight. Meanwhile, Hanan, unaware of all the preparations to save his life, developed further complications and was admitted to Nile Hospital, Kecherry, Thrissur. But all the efforts to get little Hanan back to life failed and he flew to the land of all well-being and no illnesses and was counted among the heavenly angels. Though Hanan's life could not be saved, it is accepted by all that the services being rendered by Ambulance *Koottayma* to save the lives of those on the verge of saying goodbye to life is praiseworthy. (Deepika , 06.10.2017)

"Do not save what is left after spending
but spend what is left after saving" (W. Buffett)

******

Brave-Heart Mayur Shelkhe

The Ministry of Indian Railways tweeted on 19 April 2021: "At Vangani Station of Central Railways, Mayur Shelkhe risked his life and saved the life of a child just in the nick of time. We salute his exemplary courage and utmost devotion to duty." Union Railways Minister Piyush Goyal also took to Twitter to praise Shelkhe: "Very proud of Mayur Shelkhe, Railwayman from the Vangani Railway Station in Mumbai who has done an exceptionally courageous act, who risked his own life & saved a child's life," his post read. The incident took place around 05 pm on Saturday, 17 April 2019. In a 29-second video of the incident shared by the Central Railways' Mumbai division, a 30-year-old woman, who is blind, is seen walking with her six-year-old son on the platform when the child slipped and fell accidentally into the railway tracks. Mayur Shelkhe is seen rushing towards the child and pushing him back onto the platform just in time before the express train enters the platform at Vangani Railway Station.

Mayur Shelkhe (30), the Good Samaritan of the Indian Railways told The Indian Express: "I saw the Udyan Express heading towards him. A thought just hit me that I have to save his life and I started running towards him. Within seconds I got scared and thought of backing out. I even slowed down and tried to get away from the track. But I did not want to see him being crushed under the train and started running again." Our hero Shelkhe stays in Neral with his parents, wife and a 10-day-old baby boy. When asked how his family reacted to his heroic deed, Shelkhe said, "I did not inform them for two days. But when the video went viral, they called me up. At first, my mother scolded me, but later, she said she was proud of what I did. My wife got scared and was very angry with me. She said I should have thought of them first. But she is happy now." (Express Web Desk, New Delhi, 19.04.2021)

"Don't just think, do." (Horace)
******

Achu Sailed Back to Life, Thanks to Bijo

Two-year-old Achu, the son of the Roy-Anitha couple, was playing in the courtyard with his elder brother Rubin, studying in Std. II. A bit tired of playing with his brother, Achu ran off to look for something more exciting without the elder one noticing him. The toddler ended up falling into a waterlogged paddy field, almost looking like a lake, at Kadampamkari. Achu's mother was in the kitchen and did not notice the future Gold Medalist in 1000 mts. race had disappeared from the tracks assigned to him. Meanwhile, Bijo Babu came with tea and snacks for his father, who was with his flock of ducks exploring the area and picking nitbits from the water to fill their stomachs for the day. He saw something stirring in the water and on a closer look at the disturbed waters, he saw the face of a little one struggling for breath. He immediately jumped into the watery field and came up, carrying the frightened Achu in his arms. Thundithara Babu-Renjini couple's son Bijo Babu, a Plus One student at the Vocational HSS, Thalavady, Alappuzha, was an angel guardian sent by an all-caring God to save another little angel. *Hai Bijo, we salute your brave and caring heart!* (Manorama, 28.04.2021)

"You begin saving the world by saving one person at a time"
(C. Bukowski)
******

Anay was Safe in Angel's Hands

Angel Maria Joy, daughter of Joy Abraham and Lithiya (Nidhiya) of Thrissur, won the National Bravery Award - Ekalavya Award - established by the Indian Council for Child Welfare (ICCW) for rescuing a three-year-old boy from drowning in a canal at Ramavarmapuram. The award consists of a citation and Rs.75,000/- Moreover, the Council will bear the expenses of the awardee's school education.

But how, when and where did Angel prove her bravery? Angel's neighbor three-year-old Anay, fell into a canal near the house. Angel, who was at home, heard the cry of the children who were with Anay and she ran to the place from where the cry was heard. She saw Anay floating in the canal, almost on the point of being swallowed up by water. Without a second thought about her safety or about her ability to lift Anay, Angel jumped into the water and brought him safely to the banks of the canal. Angel is a Std. V student of Devamatha CMI Public School, Thrissur, run by the Carmelites of Mary Immaculate (CMI). Angel's brothers Jewel and Abel Chris are students of Std. VIII and Std. I respectively. Hello Darling Angel, you have proven yourself worthy of your name!

The other Ekalavya Award winners are: Shanis Abdulla (Std. VII, Kozhikode) rescued a little girl from the attack of a bull; Shivakrishnan (Std. X, Wayanad) saved a child from drowning in the river; Sheethal Shashi (Std VIII, Kannur) saved the lives of three people from drowning in a pond by using floating cans; Rithujith (Std. IX, Malappuram) helped a laborer who was stuck on a coconut tree to come down safely. (Manorama, 15.02.2022)

"Courage is resistance to fear, mastery of fear, not absence of fear." (Mark Twain)

******

A Selfie That Went Awry

Vinu Krishnan (25) of Paravoor, Chathannoor, Kollam and Sandra S. Kumar (19) of Parippally were to be married on 09 November 2022. On the previous day, they decided to have an outing together without much fanfare and commotion. They headed towards Vilavoorkonam and climbed up the side of a high quarry wall next to Ayiravilly temple to take a selfie for the photo album. Sandra's grip on a protruding rock failed and she fell into a pond 150 ft. deep, with water 50 ft. high. Without a second thought for his safety, Vinu jumped in and caught hold of Sandra's dress with one hand and stayed there, gripping the side of the rock with the other hand. For about one and a half hours, the soon-to-be-married Vinu and Sandra were hanging between life and death, crying out for help. The quarry workers who heard the cry for help reached the place. They threw down a rope for the duo to hold on. Meanwhile, a few neighbors reached the spot in a country boat. Fire force and police followed. Finally, with the combined efforts of all, Vinu and Sandra were brought to safety. There was no other choice but to postpone the much-awaited wedding day. (Manorama, 09.11.2022)

"Life is a gift. Never take it for granted."
(Sasha Azevedo)
****

Ambujakshan Won in Reverse Gear

The visuals of an encounter of a private bus with a rogue elephant named Kabali with challenge-me-if-you-can written in capital letters on its forehead went viral on social media on 16 November 2022. The enervating, exciting, face-to-face Ambujakshan-Kabali meeting took place on the Valparai route in Chalakudy, Thrissur. In the video, believed to have been shot by some passengers, the jumbo could be seen coming from the opposite direction of a private bus. The private bus servicing the Chalakudy-Valparai route was stopped by Kabali, the strong elephant of the forest at Ambalapara. The driver of the bus, Ambujakshan, had to go in reverse gear as the road was narrow and congested, with no space to turn around. An experienced veteran driver, Ambujakshan was calm and braced himself up for a daunting feat and maneuvered the vehicle in backward gear and negotiated sharp curves and bends on the wild road for over eight km with the animal chasing the bus right in front of him. It was a race for life - the bus in backward gear and the tusker in forward gear - which continued until the tusker, defeated and humiliated, gave up the chase. The driver's alert and deft driving helped to save the lives of over 40 passengers on the bus. As many as nine vehicles, including two KSRTC buses and two private buses, were stuck on both sides. The bus reached Anakkayam safely and everyone heaved a sigh of relief and Ambujakshan was drowned in congratulations and hip. . .hip hurrahs. Kabali, the defeated contestant in the race, went back to the forest after reaching Anakkayam with his pride scratched a little. "It was an unforgettable experience...everyone was gripped with fear. . .there was no way other than taking the bus in reverse gear for over eight km," Ambujakshan said. Residents said the tusker had been frequenting the place for over two years. The locals named him Kabali after the title character of a Rajinikanth movie of the same name. (Deepika 17.11.2022)

Life is a daring adventure or nothing at all" (Helen Keller)

******

A Salute to Harikumar and Harisudhan

Whether young or old, girls or boys, it is difficult to reject the tempting invitation of Thanmadi Pond near Dharmasastha Temple, Kurattikad, Mannar, to have a dip in its cool, clean waters. So, the passers-by were not surprised when they saw six boys having a good time in the pond. But soon, the pleasure dip turned into a fear dip as the two of them started sinking into the water. Their companions raised a hue and cry and desperately called out for help. Not far from the temple, two laborers, Harikumar and Harisudhan, who were engaged in making a shed, heard their desperate cry and ran to the spot only to find the duo almost on the point of being swallowed by the merciless waters. They threw themselves into the water, caught hold of the frightened, sinking teens and brought them safely back to the shore. Their family members were unaware of the happenings since the adventure-seeking teenagers had left the house without informing them of their intention to have some playtime in the pond. When told about the event, they had only words of thanks for the rescuers, Harikumar and Harisudhan. "It is common that school children, college students and others regularly come to the pond to have a dip and swim. Since the pond is quite deep, there should be a warning notice to the visitors," said the temple authorities. (Deepika, 22.11.2022)

Mahadevan-Sreeja Rendezvous

How and where was the rendezvous? Here is the story. At a time when COVID-19 was still continuing its victory march over helpless humans, K.C. Sreeja, Project Officer of the National Institute of Oceanography (NIO), who was riding her two-wheeler on the railway over-bridge in Vyttila, was knocked down by an oncoming car, at 07.30 am on 10 January 2022. The vehicle that knocked her down and a number of other vehicles that followed passed by, undisturbed by the sight of a young girl lying bathed in blood on the road. Mahadevan, a daily wage earner who was walking under the over-bridge, heard the car-two-wheeler collision noise above and ran to see what had happened. He saw Sreeja lying on the footpath, bleeding and unconscious. He lifted her to his shoulders and moved towards the road when a passing vehicle stopped and transported her to the hospital. For 15 days, Sreeja was unconscious in the ICU. Two head surgeries brought her back to consciousness, but memory played hide and seek with her for many months after she left the hospital. As Mahadevan had given his mobile number in the hospital, Sreeja was able to contact him later. In the first week of December 2022, Sreeja met Mahadevan at his residence with a heart full of thanks to her invisible God above and to

Mahadevan (means Great God), her visible God below, who brought her back to life. (Manorama, 07.12.2022)

"Courage is Adversity's Lamp." (Luc de Clapiers)
******

Nandu @ Athijeevanam

"Nandu faced cancer with unbelievable courage and encouraged people to be strong in difficult times. He motivated many through his love and kindness. His death is a loss to Kerala. I join in the pain of his family and friends. Condolence to his bereaved family members!" So wrote Chief Minister Pinarayi Vijayan on Facebook after hearing of the death of Nandu Mahadevan (27), an amputee cancer patient.

Nandu was diagnosed with cancer in 2016, at the age of 24 and his leg was amputated during a treatment at the Regional Cancer Centre in TVPM in 2018. Though initially, it was beyond his ken to understand the why of it, he decided to fight it and send out a positive message of survival against cancer. Johnson Samuel of Vettiyar provided him with an artificial leg from a German Company named Ottobock. About this, Nandu wrote on Facebook: "Next Wednesday is my wedding. The eldest daughter of a German gentleman is my bride." Immediately, the post went viral. He formed the collective Athijeevanam, through which he campaigned to help those suffering from various illnesses and financial constraints. From singing songs to sharing his thoughts, Nandu never missed a chance to send positive vibes to cancer patients through his social media page. Crowdfunding was the means he adopted to help those running short of money for treatment. Finally, when his hospital expenses soared sky-high in August 2020, he sought financial help from his well-wishers and they donated generously. After getting Rs.50,00,000/- he wrote on Facebook, "Enough! Enough! I am overwhelmed by your love and affection." He promised that he would give the remaining amount to those who needed it. On 09 April 2021, Nandu informed his followers on Facebook that his health had deteriorated and that medicines won't be effective for treatment thereafter. "Unbearable pain is there in my body, but I can stand straight and say: Life is a fight." Nandu was the face of hope and survival for cancer patients through his inspiring thoughts on social media and through his campaigns to help others. After he succumbed to the disease in the early hours of 15 May 2021 at MVR Cancer Centre and Research Institute, Kozhikode, social media was flooded with condolences as his smiling face was an inspiration for many. Nandu is survived by his parents Hari and Lekha and siblings, Ananthu and Saikrishna.

The story does not end here. Following his oft-expressed wish that after his departure, his German bride (artificial leg) should be given in marriage to a needy person, his parents donated it to Justin of Kozhikode. Nandu, you are a divine messenger of love and hope. Long Live Nandu Mahadevan! (Manorama, 10.12.2022; Google)

"Hard times don't create heroes. It is during the hard times the hero within us is revealed." (Bob Riley)

******

Vijaykumar is Helping Kumar

Vijayakumar means the Son of Success. We do not know much about Vijayakumar and how successful he has been up to 29 December 2022. On this day, with his presence of mind, courage and a certain built-in dedication to the cause of those in need, he performed a successful rescue operation. Here is how it happened. Navaneeth Krishnan and his wife with two children were out enjoying the Christmas holidays and reached Kuttyalam to have a look at the beauty of the place and feel the cool breeze caressing their faces. Leaving the kids in a place meant for the children to enjoy a dip in the cool waters, Krishnan and his wife went up to have a full view of the waterfall. Meanwhile, Hirani (4), who was having a good time swimming and playing in the water, was caught in a whirlpool and was struggling for breath. A few women who were nearby saw the little one almost drowning and they raised a hue and cry. Hearing the desperate cry of the women, Vijayakumar of Thoothukudi, who happened to be a little away, rushed to the spot, threw himself into the treacherous waters and daringly rescued the frightened little one from the murderous whirlpool. With a few injuries, Hirani was safely handed over to her parents and was admitted to the hospital. Meanwhile, our Helping Kumar left the venue without waiting for congratulations and thanks. Dear Vijaykumar, may you continue to be a blessing to your fellow humans in their hour of need! (Manorama, 30.12.2022)

"You can't live a perfect day without doing something for someone who will never be able to repay you."
(John Wooden)

******

Becks is Alive, Thanks to Yusuf Ali

"Since Shri Yusuf Ali (Yusuffali) was directly involved, I was hopeful that I might escape capital punishment. This is my second life. I'm thankful to Yusuf Ali, who has been pursuing the case and negotiating with the victim's family over the past several months," Becks Krishnan (45) told reporters outside Kochi airport. Becks (meaning stream) Krishnan is a native of Puthenchira, Thrissur. The name Becks was given to him by his father, Krishnan Shanku, in honor of his German friend. Becks graduated as an automobile engineer, found a job in Abu Dhabi, married Veena and fathered a son Adwaith and his life was flowing like a gentle stream. But it all changed in September 2012, as he was driving to Musaffah to attend a job-related meeting. He lost control over the wheel and the car ploughed into a group of kids playing on the roadside. A Sudanese boy died on the spot. Becks swore that it was an accident, but the investigators slapped murder charges on him and Abu Dhabi Supreme Court sentenced him to be executed by a firing squad. Under UAE law, the family of a person killed in a road accident is entitled to receive blood money. Once the money is deposited with the court, if the family accepts the amount and pardons the prisoner, legal proceedings are to be completed to secure the culprit's release. Becks had been languishing in

Ali Wathba prison in Abu Dhabi for seven years when Yusuf Ali stepped in. Since the deceased boy's family had returned to Sudan and settled there, Yusuf Ali had to fly to Sudan for negotiations. Ali deposited Dh.500,000 (Rs.1,00,00,000) as blood money at the Abu Dhabi court after convincing the Sudanese boy's parents to pardon Krishnan. The victim's family pardoned Becks, he was legally freed and on 02 June 2021, was reunited with his family, and Yusuf Ali lived up to his name. "It's a rebirth for me," Becks said. "I had lost all hope of seeing the outside world - let alone lead a free life." (TNIE, 10.06.2021, Wikipedia) On 13 December 2022, Manorama reported that the savior Yusuf Ali and the saved Becks Krishnan met at Nedumbassery Airport.

"Next to creating a life, the finest thing a man can do is to save one." (A. Lincoln)

******

Drum Beaters Recaptured Heartbeats

Two 11-year-olds, Aryan and Srihari, after spending some time in prayer in a temple in Ambalapuzha, decided to go for an energizing dip in the temple pond. A lady washing her clothes in the pond had seen the two getting into the water and having a good time. The rhythmic beating of the clothes on the washing stone and the giggles of the two mingled well in her ears. A little later, she realized that their laughter had stopped. Following a premonition, she raised a hue and cry and two *Panchavadyam* artists, Yadukrishnan and Vishnumon, who happened to be near the temple, heard her desperate cry and turned their steps to see what was the matter. They saw water bubbles rising from a particular site. They jumped into the pond and as they were searching for the source of the bubble about 12 feet below, Vishnumon caught hold of Srihari's legs. The two rescuers carried the frightened boy to the bank. Then, they caught sight of a set of clothes lying on the steps of the pond. They swam back to the pond and found Aryan in a very critical stage and struggling for breath and carried him to the shore. The police and the neighbors together transported the pre-teens to Medical College Hospital, Alappuzha. Aryan was later shifted to a private hospital while Srihari continued in the Medical College Hospital. Both are on the road to recovery. Aryan and

Srihari, the sons of Rajkumar and Binish of Kakkazham, respectively, are Std. V students at the Govt. Model HSS, Ambalapuzha.
(Mathrubhoomi, 23.01.2023)

"Sometimes God puts people exactly where they need to be."
(Taylor Adams)
******

Ivan is Safe in Diya's Hands

Overnight, Diya Fatima (8), the daughter of Sanal and Shajila of Mankamkuzhi, Mavelikkara, became a star and rightly so! Diya's two-year-old brother Ivan (Akku) was playing in the courtyard. As it started raining, Diya and her sister Duniya (6) went to collect the washed linen spread on the rope outside and the mother, Shajila, was washing the dishes in the kitchen. On hearing the sound of something falling into the well, Diya turned to see where the noise came from and to her absolute dismay, she saw Ivan crying out from the well 20 ft. deep. Without any further reflection or thought, Diya climbed down by the PVC pipe in the well. With one hand she lifted her precious little brother and with the other, she held onto the PVC pipe and cried out for her mother. Hearing the cry of the desperate mother and the two little ones - Diya in the well and Duniya standing out, neighbors Akhil Chandran and Binoy and guest laborer Munna reached the spot and Ivan, the fallen one and Diya, the courageous rescuer, were lifted safely out of the well. Amidst clapping of hands and cheers, Diya kissed . . . kissed . . . Ivan non-stop. The little one who suffered minor head injuries was taken to the Medical College Hospital, Alappuzha.

As the news spread, there was a flow of well-wishers to Diya's house to congratulate her for her love-laden courageous act. M.S. Arun Kumar MLA, who visited Diya, asked her if she had anything to tell him. Without batting an eyelid, she said: "A bus to go to school! Now every day, I have to walk a long way with my friends to reach the school." "By the beginning of the next scholastic year, you and your friends will ride to school in a bus." MLA's response was as quick as Diya's request. Stay Blessed, Little Great Lady Diya! (Mathrubhoomi, Manorama & Deepika dt. 05.04.2023)

"The longest journey you will ever take is 18 inches from your head to your heart."

******

Single-Minded Team Won the Day

A journey that otherwise takes over 4 hours was covered in 2.5 hours when in a heart-warming gesture, police officials, various vehicle drivers and commuters joined their heads, hands and hearts together and helped the ambulance carrying a 17-year-old critically ill girl from Kattappana, Idukki, to Kochi. Ann Maria, who enjoyed good health all along, became unwell while attending a church service on Thursday 01 June 2023, the re-opening day for Kerala schools after the summer vacation. She was immediately rushed to St. John's Hospital, Kattappana. However, after giving preliminary treatment, the authorities referred her to Amrita Hospital, Kochi, for further emergency treatment. Soon, social media was flooded with posts requesting help from the public to arrange a fast and safe corridor for the ambulance. What followed was a breathtaking attempt to save a precious life. Water Resources Minister Roshy Augustine, at the time attending a school program at Panickamkudy in Idukki, arranged an Intensive Care Unit (ICU) ambulance from Kattappana to Kochi. The SP of Idukki arranged a pilot vehicle for the ambulance. The ambulance started from Kattappana at 11.37 am took the Kattappana-Cheruthoni-Thodupuzha-Muvattupuzha-Vyttila route and reached Amrita Hospital, Kochi, in 2.5 hours.

"The successful mission was made possible by the support of the public," said Minister Roshy in an interview. "The union of ambulance drivers, auto-rickshaw drivers and bus drivers worked together to ensure a smooth and fast passage for the ambulance," he added. "The public was very cooperative. Road congestion relating to the school reopening and the long winding road from Kattappana to Thodupuzha posed a major hurdle. However, with the support of the public, we overcame every hurdle," said Subrahmanyan, the ambulance driver.

As per the hospital reports, Ann Maria's condition was considered critical. The hospital authorities extended maximum support and provided the best treatment for the girl. Her family searched for fitting words to express their gratitude to the magnanimous people and the police. The swift response and efficient coordination demonstrated by everyone involved in this life-saving mission underscore the importance of unity and solidarity in times of emergency. Ann Maria is currently (11.23 am, 02.06.2023) under observation for 72 hours in the intensive care unit (ICU) and is being treated by an expert team of doctors from the Cardiology Department. (The Hindu, 02.06.2023)

Endnote:

It is hard to contemplate what happens to us after our death. However, organ donation enables us to save the lives of others even after our final departure from our planet and we continue to live through the recipients. It provides a life-giving, life-enhancing opportunity to those who are forced to bow out of life due to vital organ failures. Moreover, it is a good way to ensure that we are lovingly and gratefully remembered even after we have said our final goodbye to our kith and kin because it is difficult for a recipient to forget the person who saved her/his life. Superheroes are not born; ordinary women and men become superheroes by their deeds of heroism and altruism. By participating in life-saving missions like organ donation or by endangering our own lives to save another life, even a complete stranger, we become superheroes.

You can save a mom or a dad or help a child survive
You can mend a broken heart and keep someone revive
Then even after you are gone, your life will happily thrive.

II
ENVIRONMENT, FOOD & HEALTH ARE TRIPLETS

According to the India State Hunger Index published by the International Food Policy Research Institute, the severity of hunger and malnutrition in Kerala is the lowest in India, though 5.6% of the total population of God's Own Country is still under-nourished. Healthy food energizes our body and mind and every cell in the body gratefully smiles back at us and is ready to face the battles ahead. According to Ayurveda, when the diet is wrong, medicines are of no use; when the diet is correct, medicines are not needed. Almost pointing an accusing finger at us, Mother Teresa said: "When a poor person dies of hunger, it has happened not because God did not take care of him or her. It has happened because neither you nor I wanted to give that person what he or she needed." In this context, it is comforting and encouraging to know that there are a few committed citizens, not necessarily rich and influential, who hear the sobs and sighs of hungry stomachs and are out there to do what they can to wipe out hunger - not from the whole world, not from Kanyakumari to Kashmir - but from their own little village or township. The following pages testify to this claim. Along with food, the environment also plays a vital role in safeguarding our health. So, in this part, Environment, Health and Food appear as Siamese Triplets.

A Green Wedding

Following the EKM District Collector's call to implement the green protocol, a unique eco-friendly marriage function was held at Perumbavoor in January 2016. The wedding of Rajesh George Joseph and Nissy Mary Joseph in an auditorium in Perumbavoor turned out to be the first green protocol function in the district. Plastic plates, glasses and bottles were not allowed at the function and all the materials used were re-usable and eco-friendly. The district administration complimented the newlyweds and their relatives and the couple was given a certificate and gifts. Municipal Chairperson Sathi Jayakrishnan, Vice Chairperson Nisha Vinayan, Suchitwa Mission representative Joshy Varghese and representatives of associations of catering also complimented the couple. Plans are off the table to promote green protocol marriages by giving gifts and certificates to the couple and to service providers like caterers, decorators etc. (DH, 13.01.2016)

"Let's nurture nature so that we can have a better future."

******

Free Rides to RCC@Auto Drivers

It's been a year since they started this novel venture. Getting to the Regional Cancer Centre (RCC), TVPM from the city railway station has always been an ordeal for patients and their relatives. Either the autos are not available when the patients arrive at the station or those present and willing charge exorbitant rates. Responding to the situation, a group of caring auto-rickshaw drivers in the city started giving free rides to patients going to RCC. The reader can meet Suresh Kumar M and his 23-member team of auto-rickshaw drivers at the Janamaitri (people-friendly) auto stand near Pettah police station. It started as two free daily rides; later, it became five. Now, the auto drivers who have formed a trust titled 'Janamaithri Auto Drivers' Koottayma' offer free rides for all RCC-bound poor patients.

"I lost my sister within one week of her getting diagnosed with cancer. We couldn't do anything then. I decided then that I would do something when I became older. When I discussed with my friends here about giving free rides, most of them were willing and thus we started this," said Suresh. A blackboard at their stand announces the names of the drivers who are ready for the day. Five auto drivers are assigned the duty each day to transport the patients. These drivers are available at the auto stand throughout the day and every ride is recorded in a notebook. They have also kept a huge banner at the Pettah railway station displaying their phone numbers and announcing free rides for RCC-bound patients. The only Janamaitri auto stand in the city is setting an awesome example with its caring drivers and their philanthropic service. For Suresh and his team, this is only a start. They are now planning to buy an ambulance to help the patients. There are many other auto-rickshaw drivers, unsung heroes, who provide free rides to poor patients. (Contact numbers: 9526385819, 8281782409. 23. 05. 2016, by Rahul.)

"Unity is strength. When there is teamwork and collaboration, wonderful things can be achieved." (Mattie Stepanek)

A Tireless Fighter Against Twisted Minds

Bezwada Wilson's earliest memory of manual scavenging is of a young member of his family telling his uncle: "Why did you give me this job? You should have given me poison instead." "I was barely four years old and could not understand why he was so upset . . . and why he smelt his hands all the time." recalls Wilson, the 50-year-old Dalit activist who has been selected for the prestigious Ramon Magsaysay Award, which details Wilson's work: "Filing PIL in the Supreme Court on the issue, raising awareness, training local leaders and volunteers for the movement. The Safai Karmachari Andolan (SKA) has liberated around 3,00,000 scavengers. The Board of Trustees recognizes his moral energy and prodigious skill in leading a grassroots movement to eradicate the degrading servitude of scavenging in India."

Wilson was raised in Karnataka's Kolar Gold Fields Township. His parents and elder brother and much of the neighborhood were manual scavengers. His early days in school were free of caste prejudices because everyone was from the same colony. But as he shifted to Kuppam, a small town about 30 km away, life became difficult and bewildering as young Wilson tried to understand what made him different from fellow students. One of his schoolmates once asked him: "Where do you live?" "In the sweepers' colony," he answered. "Till then, they were all friendly. From then on, they lost interest in me," he says. When he spoke about it to his parents, they said, "It is so everywhere; there is nothing new." In 1982, Wilson moved back to his hometown and began night classes for fellow community members to teach them to read and write. But within a short time, he realized that illiteracy was not the only problem among the Dalits. Alcoholism was another evil. Working at an alcohol de-addiction camp, Wilson learnt the bitter truth. Some people at the camp told me: "You tell us not to drink, but if you see the way we work and where we work, you will understand why we drink." His battle against manual scavenging had begun. Between 1986 and 1989, he wrote dozens of letters to authorities, including the Prime Minister of India and published articles in newspapers highlighting the scourge. Then, there was another turning point in his life. As part of Dr. Baba Saheb Ambedkar's birth centenary celebrations, Wilson participated in a cycle rally from Andhra Pradesh to Karnataka, lasting 50 days. The rallyists met hundreds of villagers on the way. It turned out to be a voyage of self-discovery. "I realized there is a word for all the discrimination I had faced. It was called untouchability, and it happened due to the caste system. And to come out of it, there was only the Ambedkar way," says Wilson. He spent much of the journey reading, listening and talking about Ambedkar's ideology.

By 1992, Wilson, the warrior against scavenging, came up with SKA, a people's movement against social evils. "I realized that the fight is not against the bucket and broom. The battle was deeper with roots in the caste system," says Wilson, a Political Science graduate. Manual scavenging was banned by an Act of the Union Govt. in 1989. Yet another Act with more bite was passed in September 2013. But the practice continues especially in Bihar, UP, MP, JK, Uttarakhand, Maharashtra and Tripura. As per the 2011 Socio-economic Caste Census,

1,82,505 households in rural areas reported themselves as manual scavengers. In the same year, House-Listing and Housing-Census found that there are about 26,00,000 insanitary latrines in the country. Sewer deaths are a recurring story of shame for India. In 2016, SKA organized a 125-day Bhim Yatra through 500 districts of various States to raise public awareness and force the government to announce a comprehensive action plan to end sewer deaths. "The entire cleaning of sewers must be mechanized. No worker should step into the drain. Stop killing us", says Wilson. He also points out that nothing changed after Bhim Yatra except for a promise to address the issues. (The Hindu, 28.07.2016)

"Concerts don't change people; rock stars don't change people. It's people that change people!"

******

A Toilet in Less than a Day

Sunita (16) of Kukkodu village near Mudigere, Karnataka, had no toilet at home when she left home in the morning to attend school in Kalasa. But a toilet was nearly ready when she returned home in the evening. The high-speed operation was undertaken by panchayat officials who were moved by the girl's teary persistence. Her father, Sheshe Gowda, had turned a deaf ear to her consistent pleading for toilet facilities for the family. Sunita narrated her story to a visiting team led by the Taluk Panchayat executive officer M.N. Gurudath. She said that she and her mother Sethu had failed to sway her father to listen to their just request. Moreover, every time they raised the issue, they got a hostile reaction. "My father drinks away his earnings," she said. The officers tried to convince Sheshe to use Swachh Bharat Abhiyan funding to construct a toilet, but he refused, leaving the girl in tears. "We were moved by the young girl's tears and decided to do it ourselves. We collected tools from the neighborhood and started digging and summoned the material needed. The girl left for school in the morning; when she returned, the toilet was nearly ready. I will never forget the joy in her eyes when she saw it," said Gurudath. The officers have decided to bear the cost of the toilet, Rs. 22,000/- and let the family keep the subsidy of Rs.12,000/- for the girl's education. Kukkodu in Kalasa Gram Panchayat has 160 households without toilets. Persistence pays! (The Hindu, 23.08.2016, Bangalore edition)

> *"Clean people and healthy people*
> *can make a wealthy country."*
>
> ******

They Gave without Counting the Cost

They could have spent their money on movies, burgers or ice cream. But Memoona Khan of Class 11 (16) and her brother Amir Khan of Class 10 (14) pooled in every penny they could lay their hands on to build a toilet for Maharani Laxmi Bai GHSS, Narsingpur District of Madhya Pradesh. For two years, they saved from the scholarship money they received as Minority Community students, to which they added Rs.2000/- from their pocket money to build the toilet. "The school had only two toilets. I felt bad to see the students standing in queues outside the toilet," Memoona, a student of Kendriya Vidyalaya in Narsingpur, told the Times of India. "I talked about it with my younger brother Amir. Since we were hesitant to discuss it with our parents, we first discussed it with our father's friend Bablu Gupta. He appreciated our concern and told our father. Luckily, our father agreed," the socially committed Memoona added. "Each of us gets Rs.2000/- scholarship annually. We'd saved two years' scholarship money in our accounts, as our father pays for our school expenses. We added to it our pocket money Rs.2000/. Thus, we had Rs.10,000/. Seeing our enthusiasm, our father also pitched in with Rs.14,500/- for the toilet," said Memoona with a We-did-it smile. The siblings' efforts were appreciated by P.K Lazarus, the principal of the school: "Around 1600 students study in our school, which had only two toilets. Now, an additional new toilet is a great relief," he said.

Memoona has contributed to other causes too. In 2011 - she was only 11 then - she wrote to Madhya Pradesh Chief Minister Shivraj Chauhan, addressing him Mamaji (Uncle) in her letter and asking him to build a road to her school. The CM responded by saying, *"Bhaanjion ki baat kaise taal sakta hoon?"* (How can I avoid talking to my niece?). Two years after writing the letter, the road was completed. Memoona has been made a brand ambassador of Lado Abhiyan, an initiative to create awareness about the girl child. The children's father, Hussain Pathan, runs a tailoring shop in Narsingpur. "Kids are very much into social activities. Memoona had even participated in a protest against an illegal liquor shop," he said.

**"Let us light the lamp of cleanliness
to spread the light of Godliness."**
******

Yuvaraj Feels their Hunger Pangs

After a day's drudgery, Saroja, a migrant laborer from Raichur, gathers her children around her at an under-construction site at Chamarajpet, an old Bengaluru area, to prepare dinner. It is only 04.30 pm, but such is their routine, early to bed, early to rise. As she begins preparation for the family's meager night meal, Yuvaraj lands at the site. He has in his hands whatever they have been craving for - vegetable pulao, plain rice, sambar and payasam. Yuvaraj M.(26), a private firm employee from Chamarajpet, didn't surprise Saroja and her hungry children. "He has come here before. Luckily, he manages to come before we cook our paltry night meal. About 20 of us, along with our children, live and work here," Saroja said. While he was handing over the food to Saroja, he got a call from N.R. Rajendra Harsha, Manager of Sankalp Banquet, to inform him about excess food at an event that could feed at least 150 people.

It all began in 2014, when at a government official's table in Kodagu, Yuvaraj saw a pamphlet with the message: "Right to Eat, Not to Waste." Inspired by this, he started this service as part of the Lions' Club Youth Wing. Since then, he has been delivering food to poor laborers who build our cities, shopping malls, roads, churches, schools and more. Yuvaraj has built a network of people who alert him whenever there is excess food. "I always felt that food should never be cooked in large quantities and wasted. I started this initiative to create awareness about judicious cooking among citizens. Now the purpose has changed and instead of cutting it short at source, many people choose to offer it for hungry laborers through me," said Yuvaraj. Heading a team of 52, Yuvaraj collects left-over food from celebration sites even at night and they fly on their two-wheelers to railway stations and construction sites where there are innumerable takers for the precious load they bring. On several days, he gets calls even after 10.30 pm. Truly a humanitarian deed that touches many lives! "Whenever Yuvaraj comes, it is a feast for us," said Kaveri, a daily wage earner. "We are working with the govt. to conduct awareness campaigns. Our aim is to celebrate World Food Day not just by providing incentives to farmers but by making a sustained

effort to reduce food wastage itself," says Yuvaraj.
(Sunday Times, 16.10.2016)

*"When people were hungry, Jesus didn't say, 'Now is that
political or social?' He said, 'I feed you'.
The good news to a hungry person is bread."* (D.Tutu)
******

Karunya Yathra is on the Way

Theruvoram Murukan, Fr. Philip Thyparambil and a few volunteers are on a *Karunya Yathra* (Mercy Tour) from Kasargod to Kanyakumari and as they move along the highways and by-ways of the State, they spread the message of love and all-inclusiveness, not by eloquent speeches or street plays or WhatsApp forwards but by their deeds of compassion and altruism. They search and find those abandoned and dejected ones on the streets, covered with muck and mire. Then, their overgrown knotted hair is cut and facial hair is shaved off. Water tanks attached to the pick-up vehicle help in the mobile bath. Thoroughly refreshing baths and freshly laundered clothes make these unwanted poor of Yahweh as normal human beings. The core message of these *Karunya Yathra* is "Mental pollution is difficult to wash off, but physical dirt can be washed off with a good bath. Clean clothes and food will do the rest. Even those living in the streets should be treated as normal human beings." The bathing, shaving and dressing take place on the roadside, not to show off but to inspire like-minded people to support the program. If any orphanage in a district is willing to accommodate them, they are admitted to such institutions. Otherwise, they are taken to the Rehabilitation Centre at EKM, run by the Social Welfare Department of the State. There are cases of the family members of a few taking them back to their homes. (Manorama, 20.10.2016)

"Life's most persistent and the most urgent question is: What are you doing for others?" (M. Luther King Jr.)
******

An Open Fridge for the Hungry

It is the Christmas season and a restaurant in Shivaji Nagar, Bengaluru, spreads the cheer and joy of the birth of Jesus among the poor in its own creative way. Mehfil restaurant, which serves Mughlai cuisine, has placed a fridge outside for the benefit of the needy. The initiative has been in association with the Rotary Bangalore Brigades. "We started 10 days ago," said Tabassum Banu, director of the restaurant, "the food inside the fridge can serve up to five persons at a time. We have also kept water bottles. So much was the demand that the staff members had to refill the fridge every 15 minutes," Tabassum said. "Like many other restaurants, Mehfil too has to deal with a lot of left-over and excess food. Most of it was being dumped. We thought that an open fridge would help us deal with food waste and at the same time feed the hungry," she added. The restaurant is conscious of the quality of the food kept in the fridge. Only the excess food in the kitchen is kept in the fridge, not what is left on the plates by the customers. The fridge is open daily from 11.00 am to 11.00 pm. One day, Lawrence, a daily wager, took a packet of biriyani to carry to his home in Nagavara to share with his family. When urged to take more, he said: "It is a gift from God. This much is enough for us." Now the Rotary District Governor has asked the 120 Rotary Clubs under him to take up this initiative," says Vimala Pinto, President of Rotary Bangalore Brigade. The city is expected to get three more fridges soon. (The Hindu, 25.12.2016)

"There are people in the world so hungry that God cannot appear to them except in the form of bread." (Gandhji)

******

A Little One with a Big Heart

In a heart-warming gesture, class II students of a private school in Rajasthan pooled money from their piggy banks to buy a wheelchair for an underprivileged, differently-abled girl. Usha, a 10-year-old girl studying in a government school in Harkewala Village, Sri Ganganagar District, Rajasthan, visited Stepping Stone English Modern School Padampur, Jaitsar Rd., Tamkot, Rajasthan, to attend a school function. Khyati, a class II student of the school, observed Usha struggling even to take a single step. After returning home, Khyati told her grandfather about Usha and inquired why she wasn't able to walk properly. Her grandfather, a retired Ayurveda doctor, explained to his concerned granddaughter the different disabilities people suffer from and added that though medical care is available, it is not within the reach of everybody. He gently suggested that if Khyati wanted, she could help the differently-abled girl by using money from her piggy bank. Khyati took up the matter earnestly and spoke to her classmates about Usha and how they could be of help to her. Wow! Soon enough, about 25-30 of her classmates were in Khyati's Help-Usha-Bandwagon. Contributions ranging from Rs.100/- to Rs.1,000/- poured in from students, parents, teachers and the management and they had enough money to buy a wheelchair.

Done! "We were happy to see the kids pooling their pocket money for a noble cause. So, we made our contributions too," said Vikas Sharma, the Director of the school. Usha's father, an agricultural laborer is deaf and mute and cannot walk properly. Google says Khyati is a name that means a great personality that engenders powerful ideas. If so, our heroine Khyati has proved herself worthy of her name. Three cheers to you, Khyati! (Hindustan Times, 25.01. 2017)

"The only ones among you who will be really happy
are those who will have sought and
found how to serve." (A. Schweitzer)
******

Help for Six Poor Girls to Tie the Knot

In a significant message to the rich who spend lavishly on opulent weddings of their daughters and sons, an ordinary fish vendor from Sullia will get six poor or orphan girls married the day his sixth daughter gets into wedlock. "With great hardships, I have married off my five daughters. My dream to help financially backward girls tie the knot will finally come true on the day my sixth daughter weds," said 56-year-old Ibrahim, the father of seven daughters and three sons. Ibrahim traveled across Sullia, Belthangadi and Puttur taluks in search of deserving brides and found six of them - two orphans and four from indigent families. His daughter's wedding will be held on 05 February 2017 at his house when the six other girls will tie the knot. Ibrahim will give them gold and clothes and treat their families with delicacies. "I am doing all these because I didn't give anything to the world when I was born, nor can I take anything when I die," Ibrahim said. "I know what it is to be poor. My mother worked in paddy fields to raise me. We were so poor that I could not even go to school," he added. In his younger days, Ibrahim went to the Middle East in search of a job. After working there for two years, he returned to Sullia and started selling fish in a tempo. Apart from sponsoring poor girls, he is involved in other charitable activities. He has donated part of his earnings to Charitable Trusts and other organizations," says Riyaz Kattekar of Malenadu Charitable Trust. (ToI, 01.02.2017)

"There is no better exercise for your heart than reaching down and helping to lift someone up." (B. Meltzer)

******

Saurabh Spreads Musical Saurabhyam

Saurabh's mission stems from the difficult times he went through in 2013 when his mother was diagnosed with blood cancer and was admitted to the cancer ward of the King Edward Memorial (KEM) Hospital, Mumbai. While attending to his mother, he noticed that most of the patients admitted there came from rural Maharashtra and were of low-income backgrounds. Their family members had left their jobs to accompany them for the highly costly treatment. "There are several Charitable Trusts that help such patients. But the problem is that money is deposited in the hospital's account in the name of the patients. Whenever a patient gets a particular medicine, the cost is deducted from his/her account. But no money goes into the hands of the relatives who also have to handle many issues connected with the treatment. If a medicine is not available in the hospital, they have to take money from their pockets to purchase it from outside," says Saurabh.

Throughout his mother's treatment at KEM Hospital, Saurabh carried his guitar to the hospital and played for the patients. His music cheered up the sad and silent atmosphere of the cancer wards. "Everybody there was worried about something or other, be it food, accommodation, availability of medicines and many other things. That's why it was nice to see that when I sang for the patients, tensions took flight, even if momentarily and the atmosphere became serene and relaxed. The doctors didn't stop me because they saw that it was having a good effect on the patients and their families," he recalled. Unfortunately, in September 2014, Saurabh's mother flew to her eternal home and he put his guitar down for the time being. Later, he decided that the time had come to pull out his guitar again. Today, he is seen inside local trains in Mumbai, with a guitar and a donation box collecting funds for the treatment of cancer patients. Employed with a pharmaceutical company, he travels by train to and from the office and on his way back from work, he belts out popular Bollywood numbers for an appreciative audience that drops money generously into his box. "In Mumbai, most people travel by local trains. So, this is the best option to reach out to the maximum number of commuters. Every time I begin with a song. When people get curious about what is going on. I explain the cause for which I am working, though I am not a good speaker," smiles Saurabh. He manages to collect about Rs.1,000/- during every trip. Though he receives bouquets and bricks, accolades and criticism from his co-passengers for collecting funds for no one in particular, he is never demotivated. You are great, Saurabh! May you continue to spread *saurabhyam* wherever life places you and may your co-humans smile because of you! (The Salesian Bulletin, March 2017)

> *"Music is the divine way to tell beautiful,*
> *poetic things to the heart."* (P. Casals)

******

Bihar's Roti Bank to Feed the Hungry

We have heard about Nationalized Banks, Private Banks, Children's Banks and so on but have we heard about a Roti Bank? Here it is! Wasting food is a terrible crime! This has been drilled into our minds ever since we were kids. Yet, we go on a wasting spree. Every single day, enormous quantities of left-over food at marriages and social gatherings are discarded as waste and what could have been a meal for the hungry turns into mere garbage. To tackle this growing problem, a group of individuals under the banner of Bihar Youth Force (BYF), a voluntary organization, has come up with an innovative campaign to form a Roti Bank, which aims to eradicate the hunger woes of the poor and to make sure that no one in the State capital goes to sleep hungry.

Rishikesh Narayan Singh's father runs a transport business in Bengaluru. His brother, a software engineer in Wipro, also stays in Bengaluru. But Rishikesh, a 26-year-old research scholar in Patna, was not lured by the lucre and decided to stay back to serve the impoverished ones in Bihar. After launching Gyandeep Book Bank, an initiative to donate books to underprivileged kids, Rishikesh vowed not to let anyone suffer because of hunger. The idea is to collect fresh chapatis (roti) and cooked vegetables from the city dwellers and distribute the same among those who are forced by circumstance to go to sleep hungry. "Initially, we plan to feed at least 100 indigents who do not have a real good meal per day. We will start from Ashok Rajpath near Patna Medical College and Hospital and cover up to Patna junction, where many people do not get adequate food. But at the same time, we will ensure that only genuinely needy people get the food as we do not intend to encourage *bhiksha-vriti* (begging)," he added. From where did he get this idea of Roti Bank? "I watched on YouTube how the Dabbawallahs in Mumbai ensured proper food to the needy. This gave me the idea to start a Roti Bank here in the State capital," Rishikesh reminisced. "About 40-50 homes have already expressed their interest to be part of the campaign and we are in dialogue with some more apartments, societies and individuals so that we can feed at least 100 people every day," says the humanitarian missionary behind the Roti Bank campaign. "The volunteer homes will be provided with two tiffin boxes sponsored by a benefactor and members of the BYF will collect packed meals every evening. They will check it for basic quality and freshness and from 08 to 09 pm, deliver the same to the poor living on footpaths, temple and hospital premises, railway stations etc. In case stale food is packed by the family, it will be given to animals, not thrown away," Singh added. "Once our efforts become successful, we will add more beneficiaries. Volunteer homes will have to fill in an application form. Only registered members will be able to donate food," he said. Registration is important as one can trace the source of the food packet in case of food poisoning. In the coming days, he intends to get schoolchildren involved in the movement. "We are in the process of holding talks with schools that can support Roti Bank. We have requested students not to waste their food. They can donate their food, if they wish so, to the needy," said Rishikesh. (DNA, 05.05.2017)

"If you can't feed a hundred people, then just feed one."
(Mother Teresa)
******

Moni Sings for the Sick

Moni's daily timetable: On every working day from 07.00 am to 01.30 pm, she works in her office. From 01.30 to 08.30 pm with a bucket in hand, Moni sings at railway junctions and traffic light junctions to collect money to help the victims of cancer and she is grateful for whatever is dropped into her bucket by kind-hearted people. The money she gets is deposited in the accounts of the cancer patients. With tears in her eyes, Moni remembers her father, who sold his watch to pay the hospital bills when she was sick and hospitalized as a school child. She has not forgotten how her brother sold the house to treat his wife who was affected by cancer. Many poor people, mostly cancer and kidney-affected patients, come to Moni for help. Recently, from her collection, she gave Rs.55,000/- to a child from Edapally who fell from a train and was gravely injured. Her favorite songs are those of S. Janaki, who is very dear to every Malayali. Moni hails from Trichur but lives in Vaduthala, EKM. Her husband Sasidharan is an auto driver, her son Avinal studies Hospital Management in Bombay and Ashna her daughter is a Plus Two student. (Metro Manorama, 29.07.2017)

"One good thing about music is that when it hits you, you feel no pain." (Bob Marley)

Johny Rests with His Canine Friends

Johny V. John Vendrapillil of Karinganchira (56), who built a farm for stray dogs in Thripunithura, EKM, was laid to rest close to his canine companions. For the last 20 years, Johny has been taking care of stray dogs, providing them shelter and food and handing them over for adoption after making sure that they would be well taken care of. It was his wish to be buried in the farm whenever death came knocking at his door. "When hundreds arrived for his funeral, none of the dogs made a noise. Usually, if they see a stranger on the farm, they bark non-stop. But yesterday, they were mourning their loss. Johny took care of them as if they were his own children," said T.K. Sajeev, Secretary of the Society for the Prevention of Cruelty to Animals (SPCA), Kerala.

Here is johny@dogstory: "After we returned from Mumbai, we rescued an injured dog abandoned in the street and opened the farm in the year 2000 to care for such wandering sick dogs. Most of the dogs that are accommodated here live in perfect harmony with the other animals," said Johny-Reena duo. In front of their 1.5-acre fruit farm at Irimpanam in Thripunithura, there is a board with the message: "Dogs Will Be Given Free." They get many calls every day either to adopt dogs or to leave the abandoned ones in the farm. The sick and disabled dogs roam around the farm carefree without anyone to sneer at them but are taken care of with much love. Johny, who is lovingly called Johny Uncle and his wife Reena cater to over 30 rescued dogs from the streets and spend their earnings for their well-being.

"Johny made sure that every new arrival was vaccinated. With his knowledge of certain dog medicines, he cured many of them," said Sajeev. "There is no place like this in Kerala. I met him a few years ago when I took to his farm six puppies that had been dumped on a hillside. I was surprised to see the dog-friendly arrangements in the farm. There was good food, shelter, a vast area where these animals could roam around freely and a couple of migrant laborers to take care of them. He was one of the greatest animal lovers Kerala has ever seen," A. Nair, an animal rights activist, reminisced. (Manorama, 21.08.2017)

"Dogs do speak, but only to those who know how to listen."
******

Cheeranchira's Own Archana

Sathish Kumar of Kunnumpurath Moolayil House, Cheeranchira, was riding a bike when an oncoming car knocked him down, which ended his earthly sojourn. His daughter Archana, who was a backseat rider, was seriously injured and was admitted to Medical College Hospital, Kottayam. To save her life, the good-hearted people of the village undertook a collection drive under the guidance of Vazhapally Village Panchayat and the Prathyasa (Hope) Team of the Archdiocese of Changanassery. From 09 am to 02 pm, the volunteers were out visiting homes, shops and institutions to collect whatever the villagers were willing or able to give to save the life of Archana, one of their own. The inborn helping mentality of the villagers rose far above the expectations of the collectors. Their target was Rs.10,00,000/- but when they counted the collected amount, they were happily and heartily surprised to see Rs.17,50,000/- in their kitty. The story is not over. Help came even from Pakistan. Bincy of Cheeranchira had sent a message via WhatsApp requesting help from her husband Biju who was working in Dubai. A few Pakistanis working in the same company heard about Archana's case from Biju and sent Rs.17.000/- which was handed over to the leaders of the volunteer group, including Fr. Sebastian Punnasserry, Director of

Prathyasa, Sunny Changankari, Panchayat President and a few others. (Deepika, 28.08.2017)

"If you are always there for others when you are in need, someone will be there for you." (J.Warner)

******

A Little One with a Big Heart

Liyana studying in Std. III in St. Francis School, Aluva, EKM, moves on the path of mercy and compassion. She had been earlier recognized and congratulated by the public, including the police, for her caring ministry of distributing food to the vagrant poor who spend their nights in her neighborhood shop verandas. She had become a little celebrity after she donated her hair, which she lovingly nurtured for four years, to help cancer patients. Now, once again, the everywhere present, everactive social media is holding her up as a Little Great philanthropist. For the past few years, the wheelchair at the Aluva railway station, meant for the physically/mentally challenged, had been in a non-functional mode. When the philanthropist Liyana heard about it, her kind-heartedness prompted her to do her bit and find a solution. She did some propaganda work among her classmates, teachers, neighbors and relatives and collected some money. To this, she added her own contribution from her piggy bank. The wheelchair dealer of EKM heard about Liyana's mission and this special item, which would have fetched him Rs.13,800 which he handed over to Liyana for Rs. 9,000. The chair has special fittings with which the sick and the old can move on the platform and reach the train either in a sitting position or lying down. On 23 June 2018, Manorama reported that the chair would be handed over to the authorities in the presence of Anwar Sadath, the local MLA and Mohammed Safirulla, the Collector of EKM, on the following day. Liyana is the precious daughter of Manarcaud Thankachan, a Cinema Production Controller and Sini, a nurse at the Palliative Care Centre of the municipality. *Li . . Liya. . Liyana, you are a noble lady!* (Manorama, 23.06.2018)

"One of the most important things you can do on this earth is to let people know they are not alone." (S. L. Adler)

******

Ponnu Mariappan is Real Ponnu

Ponnu Mariappan's workshop is on a street corner in Kolenchery, EKM Dt. and she serves the passers-by who stop by her workshop to get their broken footwear or old umbrellas mended by her expert hands. Whatever her customers decide to give her in return for her service is her only income with which she maintains her family. When Ponnu heard about the 2018 flood and the millions of Keralites who were thrown into utter despair and helplessness due to the loss of their house and means of income, her heart longed to do her bit to help the needy. When she came to know about Malayala Manorama's project Koodeyundu Nadu, to raise funds to help the flood victims, she could not pretend to be ignorant of the needs of the people. Ponnu, the mother of four children, knows very well what it is to be hungry and have no food. From her meager savings, with a motherly heart and a fervent prayer, she deposited Rs.1,000/- in the Manorama Charitable Trust Fund established for the post-flood relief works. Ponnu, who resides in the settlement colony of Ezhipram, reached Kerala from Tirunelveli, years back as a tiny tot. *Dear Ponnu, you do not possess gold and jewelry, but you definitely have a Heart of Gold!* (21.08.2018)

******

A 'Hero' for Our Heroine

"One good turn deserves another" or "Some act of kindness may bring an avalanche." Anupriya (Class II), daughter of K.C. Shanmuganathan from Villupuram, Tamil Nadu, had managed to save Rs.8,246/- over a span of four years to buy her dream cycle and proudly cycle to school. But when she watched the TV visuals on the unspeakable sufferings of 2018 flood-hit victims, her generous heart whispered to her: "The dream of owning a bicycle could wait, but the needy in the flood-hit areas should not be made to wait to get the minimum necessities of life to hold their body and soul together." So, she broke open her five piggy banks and added something more to her savings and made it a round figure of Rs.9000/- and donated the entire amount to the Chief Minister's Flood Relief Fund (CMFRF). "I wanted to buy a bicycle for my birthday in October. I had been saving money for four years. But I decided to donate my savings to the people of Kerala after I watched the destruction caused by floods on TV. I am happy to help people. I can buy a cycle later," said Anupriya.

The heart-warming gesture of the little girl came to light when someone posted this rare example of unconditional compassion and munificence on Twitter and good-hearted people couldn't stop appreciating such a young girl's understanding of the difficulties of others and her benevolence. Touched by her selfless action, Hero Cycles came forward to appreciate her not merely by words but in action. The company presented Anupriya with a brand-new cycle. "Dear Anupriya, we appreciate your gesture to support humanity in its hour of need. You would get a brand-new cycle from us. Please contact us at customer@herocycles.com," Pankaj Munjal, MD of Hero Cycles, tweeted. "Thanks to you, dear Anupriya! I have read that every act of kindness has a ripple effect. Through you, I experienced it. You are truly blessed!" said another tweet. *Magnanimous Anupriya, may your love for the suffering humanity grow with you and spread its fragrance far and wide.* (Manorama, 21.08.2018)

***"Give Thoughtfully, Enthusiastically,
Voluntarily, Cheerfully!"***

******

Mohanan is a Donor, Not a Beggar

Before the killer virus, COVID-19 shook the world nations, including India, to its foundations, there was a killer flood@2018 that convulsed Kerala's socio-politico-economic life as never before, causing death and destruction all over. For those affected by the flood, life came to a stand-still, a temporary full stop. But there were many silver linings in the darkest clouds gifted by the flood.

Mohanan of Kallekulam, Poonjar, walked four km. to reach the house of the Municipal Chairman T.M. Rasheed. Since Mohanan, a beggar, made a regular appearance at his house to ask for alms, Rasheed took out a Rs.20 note from his pocket to give him. Meanwhile, the visitor emptied his small purse in front of Rasheed and counted - two rupee notes, two rupee coins, five rupee notes, and five rupee coins - all added up to Rs. 94. While Rasheed kept wondering what the visitor was up to, Mohanan, the donor, pushed the whole amount towards Rasheed and said: "Sir, send this to the Flood Relief Fund of our CM. I do not know how to send it. Let someone in the camp have at least a cup of tea." He who was used to the endless lamentations of his famished stomach gave all he had to smoothen the hunger pangs of his co-humans in his own Big Way and leaving his hearty contributions in front of the Municipal Chairman, left the place without much ado. Mohanan, who was a mahout earlier, was hurt in an attack by the elephant he was riding and due to the inability caused by the attack, he lost his job and took to begging to keep body and soul together. *How shall we address Mohanan? A Good Samaritan? Selfless Donor? Humanitarian?* (Deepika, 01.09.2018)

"Give, but give until it hurts." (Mother Teresa)
******

A Hair Cutting Saloon for a Day

Girish Narayanan, *Chils Gents' Beauty Parlour* owner, his son Ananthu Girish, and friend Rajappan Pathirackal established a temporary Hair Cutting Saloon in front of the collectorate in EKM. Don't jump to conclusions! They were not protesting against anything. It was in response to Kerala CM's urgent call for a collection drive to help the 2018 flood victims. From 10 am to 05 pm, they served their customers and the amount collected was handed over to the village officer of Kakkanadu to be sent to the Chief Minister's Flood Relief Fund. Earlier, the above team had caught the attention of the media and the public by rendering free haircuts and shaves for flood victims in places like Kalamboor, Paravoor, Alangad, Asari Vallom Colony, etc. (Deepika, 12.09.2018)

"Service to others is the rent you pay for your room here on Earth." (M. Ali)

******

Riyas and Food Task Force

Riyas was born with a deformed arm. But that did not stop him from his studies or entering politics or stretching out his deformed hands to those in need. A practicing lawyer at Alappuzha court, the 42-year-old Riyas from Mannancherry is the *Jeevathalam* (heartbeat) of the poor in Mararikulam. With the wholehearted support and cooperation of many generous individuals, he has been helping to feed deserving, hungry people twice a day for the past three years. As convenor, he coordinates the activities of the *Jeevathalam* Pain and Palliative Care Society (JPPCS), which has spread its wings across Muhamma, Aryad, Mannancherry and Mararikulam South Panchayats. "Under this project, food is served at the doorstep of the needy by volunteers," says Riyas. Hunger-free Mararikulam Project was started in December 2017 under the guidance of former Finance Minister T.M. Thomas Isaac. "We found that many people from our area were struggling to get one proper meal a day. Many are elderly citizens who don't have children or close relatives to care for them," said Riyas. The JPPCS is now a multi-armed organization with around nine other organizations functioning under it and all of them ministering to the malnourished in the area. His friends, well-wishers and beneficiaries reciprocated his generosity by handing him victory from the Aryad division to the Alappuzha District Panchayat election on an LDF ticket. *Well Done, Riyas! May your tribe thrive!* (Sunday Express, 20.12.2020)

"You pray for the hungry. Then you feed them. This is how prayer works." (Pope Francis)

******

Olivea's *Vishukkani* for 'Uncle' Sunil

The Malayalam word *kani* literally means "that which is seen first"; Vishukkani means that which is seen first on the day of Vishu. Arranged in the family pooja room on the night before by the mother of the family, the Vishukkani is a panorama of auspicious items, including images of Lord Vishnu, flowers, fruits, vegetables, clothes and gold coins. The devotees believe this *kani* would bring them prosperity throughout the New Year.

When the 8-year-old Olivea of Pattikkad, Thrissur, came to know that her neighbor Uncle Sunil Kumar, a kidney patient, was in dire need of money, she knew she couldn't let the 48-year-old uncle and his family suffer while the whole of Kerala would be celebrating Vishu, a day dedicated to prosperity and well-being. So, our superstar Olivea decided to do her bit in consultation with her parents. Knowing that in families celebrating Vishu, *kanikonna* (Cassia fistula), a widely grown ornamental plant in tropical and subtropical areas, occupies a five-star position, a can't-do-without stature, Olivea walked around the neighborhood and collected *kanikonna* flowers. The day previous to Vishu, Olivea, the budding social worker, occupied a bit of a roadside near her house and displayed a sign board that read: *Kanikonna* for Sale. The amount collected will be used to support a kidney patient. Soon enough, her flower basket got empty and her purse giggled with fullness and Olivea counted Rs.1,850, a significant amount if one remembers that it is the fruit of the labor of love, put in by a tiny tot.

On the day of Vishu, as Olivea handed over the amount to her ailing Uncle Sunil Kumar, there was no photographer to catch the grateful, appreciative smile of the family members and the I-did-only-a-little-bit feeling of Olivea, the golden-hearted daughter of Joby and Blessy, Chuvannamannu, Pattikad. It is likely that Blessy, the mother of Olivea, soliloquized many times: *"This child of mine is a true blessing!"* Joby is an auto-rickshaw driver and Blessy works in Israel. *Hai Darling Olivea, may many more people smile because of you!* (Indian Express, 14.04.2021)

> **"It is not how much we give, but how much love**
> **we put into giving."** (M.Teresa)
> ******

Ra. . .Raja. . . Rajappan Divyang

Out of sheer curiosity, photographer Nandu K.S. approached a man rowing a   boat filled with plastic bottles and collecting more from Vembanad Lake as he moved on. Nandu was shocked beyond words when he realized that the elderly man N.S. Rajappan was paralyzed below his knees. Rajappan told Nandu that he was earning a small income by selling these thrown-away items and also helping to keep the lake clean.

While the 70-year-old sentinel of environmental health continued with his daily duty, living in a dilapidated tent near the lake, unbeknown to him, his story went viral. Rajappan's exemplary work was highlighted nationwide after Prime Minister Narendra Modi mentioned him during an episode of Mann ki Baat. "I have news from Kerala that highlights our responsibilities. In Kottayam of Kerala, there is an elderly Divyang N.S. Rajappan Saheb. Though he is paralyzed and unable to walk, his commitment towards cleanliness has not been diluted. For the past several years, he has been taking out his country boat to Vembanad Lake and collecting plastic bottles thrown by visitors. Taking a cue from Rajappanji's deeds, we must also do whatever is possible to maintain cleanliness," Modi said on air. In response, Rajappan said that he was so happy that the PM had acknowledged his efforts. Days after Modi hailed his efforts to clean the lake despite physical challenges, Rajappan was given a mechanized boat. Taiwan honored him by awarding The Supreme Master Ching Hai International's World Protection Award and a $10,000 (about Rs.7,30,081/-) cash award and a citation.

Rajappan has been afflicted by polio from the age of five and he is dependent on his sister's family to meet his daily needs. Rajappan is a real Raja - King in his own way! (The Hindu & Deepika, 01.02.2021; Mathrubhoomi, 04.02.202)

> *"You have environmental problems?*
> *Stopping pollution is the best solution."*
> ******

Sabeesh is on a Cleaning Mission

Inspired by the example of Rajappan, R. Sabeesh (41) every afternoon ventures into the Parayanchal canal in front of his house at Manaveli, Thanneermukkam, on a small fiber boat and after an hour, he rows back home with a boat-load of plastic bottles, used containers and a mix of other waste matter collected from the stream. He is on a mission to clean Parayanchal and its tributaries linked to Vembanad Lake, whose role model is the differently-abled man N.S. Rajappan from Kottayam who was hailed by Narendra Modi for his efforts to clean up the lake by collecting plastic. "After the PM praised Rajappan for his efforts to clean up the lake in spite of his age and disabilities, he received a lot of attention from the newspapers, TV channels and social media. But not many people have followed his example. His efforts are worth emulating as it will clean water bodies and ensure its protection," said Sabeesh, who bought a fiber boat for Rs.26,000/- and, in July 2021, started collecting plastic floating in the water. He has so far collected more than 3,000 plastic bottles and a host of other plastic materials. "Apart from getting water bodies rid of plastic waste, I also want to prove that a kidney donor - he donated a kidney to his wife two years ago - can lead a normal life after the surgery. Rowing a boat using an oar involves a lot of physical activities," he says. Sabeesh, who runs a PSC Coaching Centre, has plans to buy a bigger boat and with the help of other like-minded environment lovers, extend his service to other water bodies, including Vembanad Lake itself, the biggest lake in Kerala. (The Hindu, 09.08.2021)

"Nurture nature and nature will nurture you." (B.D. Souza)
******

Kadapra is on a Get-Well Mission

It is an accepted fact that the contents of our money bags decide many of our choices and pursuits. When it is empty, we humans are in neck-deep trouble, whether the issue is how to keep the pot boiling, children's education, medical treatment, purchase of new clothes, marriage expenses, and the like. The people of Kadapra Panchayat, Pathanamthitta Dt. came together to prove that an empty purse need not be a problem if munificent women and men stand together and extend a helping hand to people in need. They stood united with the firm determination that no one's life should be handed over to death for lack of the seemingly all-powerful money. On Gandhi Jayanthi Day 2022, the fund collection drive was inaugurated by Fr. K.V. Paul Rabban of Parumala Seminary. Grouped into 60 squads, 600 members of Kadapra belonging to 15 wards went from house to house on a Wellness Mission and collected Rs.50,000,00/- before the sun dipped into the western horizon on the same day. The precious collection was handed over to Nisha Asokan, the Panchayath President, to be used for the kidney transplant of five youthful fellow human beings, namely: Malutty (25), Mukesh (30), Ranjith (30), Saranya (34), and Pramod (48). (Deepika, 04.10.2022)

"To ease another's heartache is to forget one's own."
(A. Lincoln)
******

A Wanderer Turned Lakshapathi

Here is a story that challenges even a high-class film thriller. M.G. Sasindran (70) of Mannar, Alappuzha, started his service to the nation as a military driver. After his retirement, he worked in SBT for some years. He changed gears again and became a lorry driver. Sometime, somewhere along the way, Sasindran's memory said goodbye to him. Consequently, he forgot his name, address, service records, pension claims etc. and wandered about as a poor beggar in Kottayam and nearby places before he ended up in a home for the destitute where goddess Luck was waiting for him. The warden of the destitute home recognized him as a former military man and accompanied him to the Defence Pensioners' Disbursing Office (DPDO). Good-hearted people helped him to get an Aadhar Card, PAN Card and Identification Certificate. When things were moving in the right direction, Sasindran's memory played tricks on him and he vanished from sight. After many days of hectic search and inquiry, some angels of charity found him in Shanti Bhavan, Kottayam. Next, Sasindran was found waiting at the bank counter, where he was welcomed and felicitated by the bank employees with a ponnada. The destitute Sasindran of Mannar, Alappuzha, left the bank counter as a Laksha-pathi, as he received Rs.21,61,000/-, his pension arrears of 16 years. "I am a person now," said Sasindran with tears of joy welling up in his eyes. He searched for words to thank Ajith Bhaskar and Mohandas, auditors of DPDO, who took the lead in tracing the wanderer Sasindran. All's well that ends well! (Manorama, 25.11.2022)

"Give to the world the best you have, and the best will come back to you." (M. Bridges)

******

Devasykutty – Oru Nalla Kutty

Velimparambil Devasykutty's heavenly patron St. Sebastian was martyred by the piercing of arrows around 255 CE by the orders of the Roman Emperor Diocletian as a punishment for professing his faith in Jesus Christ. But Devasykutty of Poomkavu, Alappuzha, proclaims his faith in Jesus Christ and lives to quell the piercing hunger arrows of the poor and the abandoned in the Medical College Hospital, Alappuzha and distributes food to those who have no one to take care of their basic needs. In Devasykutty's own words: "I am 67 years old. There was a time when I lived lavishly, splurged money right and left and was a slave to many bad habits. Then my God came to my rescue. Now, every morning, I visit the General Wards in the Medical College Hospital, carrying bread and milk. There are many poor patients who wait for me with expectations writ large on their faces. I am not left alone in this joyful task; there are many other-oriented people who help me in this poor-oriented mission."

Devasykutty follows the philosophy of the More. In the hospital, there are bed-ridden patients with no one of their kith and kin to help. So, our angel of charity washes their clothes, gives them a bath, cleans the toilet and assures them that without much delay, they will leave the hospital healthy and strong. For the last 32 years, this man who believes that faith without good works is as good as being dead has been engaged in this great work, so dear to the God of the poor. At 11.00 am on 30 December 2022, when the undersigned contacted Devasykutty, he was engaged in washing the clothes of the abandoned patients in the hospital. Yet More! In his house in Poomkavu, he has kept four beds to render temporary help to those who have nowhere to go after they are discharged from the hospital. Devasykutty's wife, Mariamma, son Shaji, daughter-in-law Lissy and granddaughter, Gloria, are ready with hands extended and hearts open wide to help him in his work of mercy. *Devasykutty is our own Blessed Kutty* (Manorama, B'luru ed. 12.12.2022)

"Food is symbolic of love when words are inadequate."
******

Sundaran Has a Sundaran Heart

Not sure whether Sundaran (Handsome) is physically handsome according to the new-gen concept of physical beauty. But the sexagenarian Sundaran is true to his name and is absolutely Sundaran in his heart and soul; therefore, Sundaran in the eyes of God and in the eyes of the poor whom he serves. He sleeps on any of the empty beds in the General Hospital in Kasargod. If no bed is free, the bare hospital floor suffices for sleep to embrace him at night. Even when asleep, the eyes and ears of his heart are open to see and feel the needs of the poor patients in the ward.

Here is the story behind the story. About 50 years ago, an unconscious 10-year-old boy suffering from epilepsy was found lying on the road. Some caring pedestrians picked him up and took him to Taluk Hospital, Kasargod and in the hospital register his name is recorded as Sundaran. For many years, he was the unofficial Ward Boy of the hospital, at the beck and call of patients, doctors, nurses, visitors and all. In 2008, the aforesaid Taluk Hospital was raised to the status of the General Hospital and the then Health Minister, Smt. P.K. Sreemathy's intervention on Sundaran's behalf resulted in the inclusion of his name in the employees' list of the hospital and now he gets his monthly meager salary from the Hospital

Management Committee Fund. Today, he is the official ward boy of the hospital. Officially or not, as before, he is a much-wanted helper to all and sundry. There is hardly anyone associated with the hospital who has not received timely help from Sundaran. His uninvited childhood friend, epilepsy, refuses to abandon its grip on him and follows him even at the age of 60+ and, at times, throws him down unconscious. But the hospital staff are there to help him through. As Sundaran is concerned about the health and well-being of the hospital staff and patients, they are equally concerned about Sundaran's health. *Hi Sundaran, by your name and by your deeds, you are really Sundaran!* (Manorama, B'lore 12.12.2022)

"The simplest acts of kindness are by far more powerful than a thousand heads bowing in prayer." (Gandhiji)

******

Mr. Joy is a Carrier of Joy

The news about more than 250 poor patients abandoned in various Govt. Hospitals in Kerala with nobody to care for them deeply touched the giving heart of Joy Kannanackal of Thiroor, Malappuram Dt., Kerala. Joy, who was running an A.C. Repairing Shop in Riyadh, Saudi Arabia and had all that was needed to live a comfortable, cozy life, left behind his business and profit and took the route of Caring Service to the hungry, sick and poor in the hospitals. He started this humanitarian service in 1995 at the Medical College Hospital in Thrissur. Even after the hospital was shifted to Mulankunnathkavu in 2005, he continued his ministry in the hospital. For the last 28 years, Joy has been a father, mother and sibling to the patients who are abandoned in the aforesaid hospital.

He is the Founder-President of a service organization known as The Friends of the Humble and coordinates the services rendered to the patients. Every morning, when Joy reaches the hospital with food for about 30 hungry stomachs, the eyes of the patients glisten with anticipated hope for a tasty breakfast. Not only food but also medicine and other needed items are supplied to the patients with the help of many like-minded people. The volunteers give baths to some, cut the unruly hair of others, wash their bed linen, clean the ward and more. When patients are discharged, if the relatives don't come to take them home, the volunteers find a rehabilitation place run by the govt. to take care of them. During the lockdown period, homeless patients were shifted to one ward in the hospital itself and were taken care of. Hospital authorities, doctors, nurses and the police are all by the side of Joy to render a helping hand whenever and wherever needed. *Dear Joy, you carry joy to the sad and lonely. You are kindness personified!* (Manorama, B'luru, 13.12.2022)

"Whoever is generous to the poor lends to the Lord and He will repay him for his deeds."
(Proverb, 19.17)
******

Doctoramma and Doctor Son

The Supdt. of Pulinkunnu Taluk Hospital sent out a request on 27 July 2022 via the District Information Service Facebook page for free service as Medical Officer, Pharmacist, Lab Technician and Data Entry Operator for a minimum period of six months in the hospital. Needless to say, trollers who have nothing else to do but keep trolling took up the matter and the idea was trolled: "Will anyone ever offer to do free service?" This sarcastic question of the jokers was answered in due time by Dr. Mathew George (43), Vachaparambil House, Pulinkunnu, whose *tharavadu* (family house) is a hop, skip and jump away from the Taluk Hospital. He joined duty in the emergency ward of the hospital with the resolution that no sick person should suffer because of the non-availability of doctors. Four months later, his mother, Dr. Grace George (69), followed in the footsteps of her doctor son and joined the hospital. Dr. George, who lives in EKM with his family, now stays in his *tharavadu* during the week, goes to EKM on weekends, and reaches back on Mondays. Dr. Grace George had served 42 years in Muscat before she returned to her native place, Pulinkunnu, two years ago, where she started a private clinic that renders free service to the needy. *Kudos to you, Mother-Son duo! May you live 100 lives!* (Deepika, 18.01.2023)

"When we give cheerfully and accept gratefully,
Everyone is blessed." (Maya Angelou)
******

Harvest is Ready & Laborers Are Many

On Saturday 21 January 2023, a group of 35 B.Ed. and M.Ed. students, mostly girls of Farook Training College, Kozhikode, reached the paddy field of Chinnettan, the 78-year-old farmer from Ramanattukara who was in great need of laborers to harvest the crop. "Chinnettan was excited when we offered to lend a helping hand to make up for the labor shortage. As members of NSS, all of us were happy to be part of the endeavor," said Nourin Sharaf, M.Ed. student who coordinated the harvesting activities. From 08 am to 12 noon, the new-gen harvesters and their sickles were in a heart-to-heart conversation with the ripe paddy plants as they harvested the crop. "Many of the group were exhausted after the five-hour work, but it taught them many precious lessons and helped Chinnettan in his efforts to conserve traditional rice varieties on leased property," added Nourin. Most of them had no previous experience with harvesting since the majority of them were from urban families who had only read or heard about harvesting. "Seeing these youngsters engaged in farming activities is a pleasure and I look forward to their continued involvement in conserving traditional agricultural practices," said Chinnettan, beaming with pride. During his interaction with the students, he recalled that the lessons he learnt from his forefathers and his passion for farming helped him protect over 10 unique rice species from extinction. The harvesting team left the field after getting hands-on experience in manual harvesting, threshing and cleaning methods and promised Chinnettan further help in his efforts to popularize rare rice varieties. *Hello, new-gen harvesters, Stay Blessed! Stay Happy!* (The Hindu, 22.01.2023)

"If agriculture goes wrong, nothing else will have a chance to go right." (M.S. Swaminathan)

******

Give and You Will Receive

The name Devan P. Vandanam of Ambalapuzha N. Panchayat is a synonym for solicitous care for the suffering humanity. If Devan is considered an ocean of mercy, his friends proved to be an ever-swelling ocean of mercy when he needed their help. When Devan was admitted to a hospital in Vaikom following a fall that resulted in a blood clot in his brain his neighbors and well-wishers decided not to let him suffer for want of money. When they were informed that the hospital treatment required around Rs.13,00,000/-, they put their hearts and hands together. Under the leadership of Jeevan Raksha Samithi (Life-Saving Association), within a few hours, they collected Rs.4,00,000/- from four wards of Ambalapuzha

North Panchayat and Rs.3,00,000/- from Neerkunnam - a total of Rs.7,00,00/- Together with other contributions earlier given by a few like-minded people, they had over Rs.10,25,000/- which was handed over to Devan's brother Mohanan by H. Salaam MLA. It was decided by Devan's friends that the collection will continue till he is discharged from the hospital healthy enough to continue his Good Samaritan activities. (Mathrubhoomi & Manorama, 14.11.2022)

But Devan is not willing to be tied to his bed. Art was very much a part of his life, even during his school days. Now, he is recapturing his artistic talents and the results are seen in his paintings on wood and cloth and in terracotta ornaments. His only daughter Devika, who has inherited her father's artistic talents, is by her dear Achhan to extend to him the necessary help and emotional support. While healthy, he supported the family with his carpentry; now, the never-say-die Devan will continue to be financially independent with his artistry and paintings. (Mathrubhoomi, 25.02.2023)

"We must be willing to let go of the life we planned, so as to have the life that is waiting for us." (J. Campbell)

******

School Children & Orupidi Nanma

V.R. Krishna Teja Mylavarapu IAS (b.1987) took charge as the 56th Collector of Alappuzha in August 2022. Ever after, he has been very much involved in getting those on the higher echelons of society to reach out to those on the periphery. Here is his mega surprise service for 2023.

Children for Alleppey - *Orupidi Nanma* (a handful of goodness) is an initiative of the District Administration that encourages children to donate food and other essentials (except rice and cash) to economically disadvantaged families. Less than a month after the program was initiated, many schools chipped in to uplift 3,613 extremely poor families in the district, identified in a govt. survey in 2022. As per the project, the first Monday of every month is observed as Community Service Day (CSD) in schools and the first CSD was held on 06 February 2023. Essentials, including food items, soap, toothpaste etc., brought by the children were segregated before being packed and distributed to adopted families. The kit to be given to the families is designed to meet the needs of the family for a month. To run the program sustainably, the student-family ratio is fixed at 100:1. The project will help the children learn the importance of sharing and caring while ensuring support to the needy. "It is a voluntary program but almost all the schools in the district, parents and children have willingly come forward to become part of this philanthropic mission. The most important aspect is that children are leading the way to make Alappuzha the first district in the country to eradicate extreme poverty," says Mr. Teja, who mooted the idea. Govt. High School, Mannancherry, with a student strength of 2,222, has adopted 22 families. "On the day fixed, the children brought all kinds of useful items and we prepared 45 kits. After distributing 22 kits to the families adopted by us, the remaining items were given to needy students and to the poor in the locality," said the HM of the school, Sujatha Kumari. For the success of the program, one teacher in each school has been given the additional charge of Community Service Coordinator. Teja in Sanskrit means strength, courage, valor, brilliance, and splendor. *Kudos to you, our Good, Great Teja! You have done justice to your name!* (The Hindu, 25.02.2023)

"We know that a peaceful world cannot long exist, one-third rich and two-thirds hungry." (J. Carter)

******

Anil Kumar is on an Urgent Mission

Located in the backwater landscape of Kottayam, the village of Enadi still retains its old charm of fresh air, singing birds, dancing flowers, caressing breeze and more. However, the Pullanthi River, a tributary of the Muvattupuzha River that flanks the village, contrasts sharply with its accumulated garbage and overgrown weeds, blocking the way to Vembanad Lake. Anil Kumar (58), a timber contractor by profession who lives on the river bank, is on a mission to restore the waterway to its former glory. Every morning, he sets sail on his country boat to clear the weeds using a sickle attached to a 10 mt. long pole. "This river used to be a favorite thoroughfare for the country boats. The overwhelming tide of garbage flow and weed proliferation gradually converted the picturesque stream to a trickle," he says. Kumar volunteered to clean up the Pullanthi River, which is the only direct access to the residents of a small islet called Cheruthuruthu. "Though the residents of our area approached the authorities with a request to clear the waterway, no funds were made available. So, I decided to clean up the river on my own," he explains.

Nearly three months into his mission, Kumar has cleared around two km. of the river stretch. Consequently, he has inspired the villagers to constitute a people's collective that has started cleaning the water body from the other end. He serves as the chairman of the collective. "A full-scale restoration of the waterway will benefit not just the local residents but hundreds of those living on both sides of the river," he adds. (The Hindu, 05.03.2023)

"Environment is no one's property to destroy;
it's everyone's responsibility to protect." (M. Agadi)
******

An Ambassador for Organic Farming

To increase crop production to meet the growing population's demand for food, unhealthy farming practices such as using killer chemical fertilizers and harmful pesticides and herbicides have been in vogue for the last few decades. While these techniques help farmers to improve their farm yield and profit, they cause food poisoning and consequent disastrous health problems affecting the lives of consumers. Ponnamma (golden mother), our heroine, has not studied or written high-flying theses about organic farming or the harmful use of chemicals in farming. But she is acclaimed as Alappuzha's Ambassador for organic farming.

Ponnamma leaves her house daily at 08 am and heads towards the homes of a few farmers in Mayithara, Mararikulam and Kalavoor, who are known for their dedication to green farming and buys *jaiva* vegetables of all kinds. Then she moves - nay flies - to her next stop, which is Mullackal market in the heart of Alappuzha town, where those who have known her for the past many years wait for her uncontaminated, pure gift of Mother Earth. Soon, the board on which her farm products are displayed gets empty and her purse wears a broad, grateful smile. The day's duty done, Ponnamma marches home by 08 pm. Not sure whether she had time to open her lunch box. Alappuzhaites know that Ponnamma considers farm products as real *ponnu* (gold) and wouldn't sell poisoned products. She is an ardent believer in organic vegetables and is aware of the known and unknown dangers of chemicals used in farming. In her younger days, she brought to the market only what she cultivated in her limited land area. When the demand for her vegetables increased, she sought out like-minded farmers who produce health-supporting vegetables. Alleppuzhaites, who value their family's health, wait for Ponnamma to download her goods in her allotted space in Mullackal Street.

Ponnamma from Kuttipurath House, North Aryad, Alappuzha, has been a permanent presence in the Mullackal market for the last 30 years or more. After her husband, Raghuvaran, said goodbye to his family 33 years ago, she took up vegetable farming and sale as a means of income. The untimely death of her son Shaji due to heart attack did not wreck her life but strengthened her determination to live and work for her grandchildren Shanu and Sharu and their mother, i.e., Ponnamma's daughter-in-law Jayamole. *Ponnamma is true to her name. Jai! Jai! Ambassador Ponnamma!!!. . . Jai! Jai Organic Vegetables!!!* (Deepika, 08.03.2023)

"With wrong farming methods, we turn fertile land into deserts. Unless we go back to organic farming and save the soil, there is no future." (Jaggi Vasudev)

******

One Heart, One Mind to Save Gopinath

Gopinath (15) from T.N. suffering from severe brain-related problems and oozing bedsores, lying on his mother's lap at Thampanoor railway station, was in critical condition. His father, Balan and sister Vijayalaksmi, were with him. When the Station Master saw him in such a pathetic condition, a do-something bell rang in his heart. Soon, Gopinath's pitiful situation was communicated to the office bearers and members of Lion's International and a few members came forward to help the ailing teen. Initially, they thought of sending Gopinath and his family by train to T.N., but the idea was gutted. Their next plan was to send them to their native village by ambulance but that idea too was vetoed. Finally, it was decided to find a place in TVPM itself to treat the suffering teenager and later pack him off to his native place. So, they approached Fr. Joseph Chacko, Vicar of St. Gregorios Orthodox Church, Nanthankode, TVPM and requested accommodation for four people for about 15 days. The answer was, "I am with you; bring them here; there is place on the second floor of the building."

Without much delay, Gopinath and his family were escorted to the above-mentioned church. Free medical services were rendered by Dr. Mini Prakash of PRS Hospital, Neurologist Dr.

Ayyappan of SUT. Plastic Surgeon Dr. Visakh Varma, Medical College Neurologist Dr. Alex Iype and others. Shiju Stanley of Care & Cure Agency took charge of the family's daily needs. Gopinath regained consciousness within two days and his health index was almost okay after 15 days of medical care.

Soon, a letter flew to the Chief Secretary of T.N. explaining the situation of Gopinath and his family. Within a few hours, a call came from Shilpa Prabhakar, the Health Mission Director of T.N., following which Gopinath was transferred to Medical College Hospital, Trichy, by an ambulance provided by I.C. Cherian, a member of the Managing Committee of Orthodox Churches and the owner of Metroscan. With food provision for 45 days and Rs.1,00,000/- received as a gift, Gopinath and his family said goodbye to TVPM with ecstatic and exuberant hearts. By evening, Gopinath was admitted to the ICU of Medical College, Trichy. Malankara Orthodox Church and the Lion's Fellowship promised help for the higher studies of Gopinath's sister.

The deeply grateful family couldn't find proper words to thank the good people of TVPM for saving their son from the clutches of death through their medical care and warmth and for making arrangements for safe transport to their native village. Verily, the Sun of Goodness shines brightly in the hearts of a few other-oriented humans! (Manorama, 22.03.2023)

"Goodness is the only investment that never fails."
(H.D. Thoreau)
******

Janardhanan, the Generous Donor

Janardhanan, a beedi worker from Kurua, Kannur, was issued a VIP card for the swearing-in ceremony of the second Pinarayi Vijayan Government held at the Central Stadium, TVPM, on 20 May 2021. He could not be part of the function as he was resting after he underwent angioplasty, so he watched the function at home on television. Why such special consideration from the CM to an ordinary man? Read on:

Chaladan Janardhanan (65), a beedi worker had set a model in benevolence in August 2021 by donating Rs.2,00,000/- to the CM's Distress Relief Fund when Kerala lay prostrate at the feet of the killer Covid-19. After his munificent act, his bank account showed a balance of Rs.850/-only. When questioned about it by the bank employees, he said: "Even today, I get enough for my life by rolling beedies. Let the money remaining unused in the bank go to someone in urgent need of the same." He strictly instructed the bank officials not to reveal his name as he wanted to remain anonymous. But some journalists got wind of his act of mercy and gave it due publicity. Janardhanan, a strong CPM supporter and a staunch fan of Pinarayi Vijayan, had said that he had donated his savings to enable the CM to fulfill his word of providing vaccines free of cost to all in the State. Janardhanan, who started rolling beedies at the young age of 13, had worked at Dinesh Beedi, Kannur, for around four decades. His wife Rajani, who was also an employee of the Beedi Cooperative, passed away in June 2020. He made the praiseworthy donation from his retirement benefits, the gratuity amount of his wife and the monthly disability pension he received. *Hai Janardhanan Saheb, you have proven yourself worthy of your name!* (Mathrubhoomi, 14.04.2023)

"Those who give, have all things.
Those who withhold, have nothing." (Indian proverb)
******

Thim. . Thimi. .Thimithom . . Thimmakka!

Saalumarada Thimmakka, the most prominent environmentalist from Karnataka who has earned the sobriquet of *Vriksha Matha* (Mother of Trees) for planting 8,000 trees, including 384 banyan trees, was honored along with other personalities at Rashtrapati Bhavan on 16 March 2019. In a ceremony marked by strict protocols, Thimmakka, dressed in a light green sari, with a smiling face and *tripundra* on her forehead, approached the dais to receive the award from President Ram Nath Kovind. As the president, 33 years younger than Thimmakka, asked her to face the camera, the centenarian Thimmakka touched his forehead to bless him. Her innocuous move brought a smile to the faces of the president and all the guests who were present burst into rapturous applause for her.

President later claimed it as a privilege. "It is the president's privilege to honor the best and the most deserving Indians. But today I was deeply touched when Saalumarada Thimmakka, an environmentalist from Karnataka, and at 107 the oldest Padma Awardee this year, thought it fit to bless me," President Ram Nath Kovind wrote on Twitter.

Thimmakka, who was born into a farming family in Hulikal village in Karnataka, who has scripted an inspiring story of grit and determination, celebrated her 111th birth anniversary on 30 June 2022 at Dr B. R. Ambedkar Bhavan in Bengaluru. As a teenager, she was married off to Bikkala Chikkaiah. They were a happy, hardworking couple living a very ordinary life. As the couple was not blessed with children, prayers, rituals and pilgrimages became part of their daily schedule and planting banyan tree saplings was one such ritual. What started as a prayerful routine to have the good fortune of having children turned out to be a caring relationship with these little green plants. The couple shot to fame for planting and nurturing about 384 banyan saplings along a four km. Highway stretch, between Hulikal and Kudoor village, near Chikkaiah's native place in Tumakuru, which grew up to be giant trees forming cooling canopies over the passers-by. After her husband said goodbye to her and their ever-flourishing children in 1991, Thimmakka, the Environmentalist, carried on the mission by herself. In total, she has planted over 8,000 trees during a period of 65 years. For her work, she won the National Citizen Award from the Government of India, the Karnataka Rajyotsava Award, and Hampi University's Nadoja Award among many other national and international awards. Silviculturist, Environmentalist, and 'Mother of Trees' are all titles she has in her kitty. Thimmakka was honored with a Cabinet Rank by Karnataka CM Basavaraj Bommai on 30 June 2022, her 111th birth anniversary and was also made an Environment Ambassador.

Despite the laurels, awards, titles and media coverage, Thimmakka's fame never translated into any material fortune. She lived in a hut till the Karnataka State Government built a house for her in 2014. Thimmakka's story is that of a woman who had to deal with a society that devalued women and instigated verbal violence (if not physical) for her reproductive inability. Thimmakka luckily had an understanding spouse who stood by her through thick and thin and they moved together on the path of tree planting and protection. (Mathrubhoomi, 04.06.2023, Website Vinay Kumar V)

******

The Seed Mother Rahibai Soma Popere

Inventive Farmer and Conservationist Rahibai Soma Popere of Mahadev Koli community (b:1964) hails from Kombhalne village, Akole block of Ahmednagar, Maharashtra. Though she has had no formal education, she pioneered a movement to preserve indigenous seeds with the help of the Bharatiya Agro Industries Foundation (BAIF), an organization promoting sustainable livelihood in rural India and helping farmers cultivate native varieties of crops. Rahibai has an extraordinary understanding of crop diversity and on her farmland, she grows 17 different crops. Raghunath Mashelkar, the erstwhile Director General of the Council of Scientific and Industrial Research, gave her the honorific title of The Seed Mother.

An active member of the Self-Help Group (SHG) of Kalsubai Parisar Biyanse Sarvdhan Centre (Committee for Seed Conservation), Rahibai has to her credit the development of a series of hyacinth beans for SHGs and families in nearby villages. She has her own creative methods of water harvesting, thus turning wastelands into productive lands. She trains farmers and students on ways to select seeds, maintain the fertility of the soil and control pests. She is skilled in four-step paddy cultivation, namely: preparing the land, transplanting the paddy seedlings, maintaining the field and harvesting. She rears poultry in her yard with the support of the Maharashtra Institute of Technology Transfer for Rural Areas (MITTRA).

In January 2015, she received appreciation from R. R. Hanchinal, Chairperson of a government body for the protection of Plant Varieties and Farmers' Rights in India. She was visited by the BAIF Development Research Foundation in 2017, which found the gardens she supported had enough produce to meet the dietary requirements of a family for a whole year. Rahibai was awarded Nari Shakti Puraskar, instituted by the Ministry of Women and Child Development, Government of India, in 2018. Every year, BBC 100 Women, names 100 influential and inspirational women around the world and shares their stories and

Rahibai was among the three Indians on the BBC List 2018. Padma Shri, one of India's highest civilian honors was presented to her by the President of India, Ram Nath Kovind, in 2020. Other awards are The Best Seed Saver Award and the BAIF Development Research Foundation Best Farmer Award. (Wikipedia)

"To forget how to dig the earth and tend the soil is to forget ourselves." (Gandhiji)

******

Hungry? This Way, Please!

An unusual display board in front of a house by the side of Kellakadavu-Venmoni road says: Welcome if You Are Hungry! Here is the caring-sharing story behind the welcome board which was placed there five months ago. The inner push for this humanitarian decision came to Pastor M.A. Philip of the Assemblies of God Church, Kodupunna, Chengannur, Alappuzha, when he was traveling with his family. As he casually looked out of the window, he noticed some ill-dressed, malnourished people on the roadside and heard a few unspoken words: "Why don't you do something to assuage their hunger?" It was an irresistible inner call to listen to the silent cry of the undernourished and famished children of Yahweh. When he shared his intimate soul experience with his wife Sophy and sons Jabesh and Johns, they supported the idea wholeheartedly. Hence, the aforementioned board was placed in front of the Pastor's Manatharayil House. So far, the family has served over 50 people craving for food. Ever after, no hungry person has passed that way without answering positively to the wailing of his/her aching, empty stomach. If the already-cooked food is over, the welcome guests will have to wait till fresh food is cooked and served. Pastor Philip and his family will hear the words: "I was hungry and you gave me to eat" from the Lord of Heaven when they knock at the Pearly Gates. (Manorama, 11.06.2023)

"God does not create poverty; we do, because we do not share." (M. Teresa)

******

Drink the Beverage & Eat the Cup

As the menace of plastic waste has reached Himalayan proportions, giving remedy-less, permanent headache to the general public at large and as healthy, speedy disposal of the same seems unreachable, a few Start-Uppers in Kerala and Karnataka have found a feasible and enjoyable alternative to plastic and zero waste. Now, those interested can taste their edible cups together with their favorite hot or cold beverages. These edible cups are manufactured and marketed by a Start-Up floated by a team from Mangaluru (Karnataka) and Kerala and are sold under the brand name Enchi Crunchi in Karnataka and Rosma Biscuit Cup in Kerala; the latter is also the name of the Start-Up. "The cups are made out of millets, the main ingredients being ragi, jowar and rice," Deekshit Vijaya, a member of the Start-Up, told The Hindu. The cups are available in two variants: hot and cold. "It's all about having good taste. The customers can pull up a chair, sit comfortably and take a hot beverage of chocolate, cardamom, vanilla and biscuit-flavored cups. If the customer votes for the cold beverage, they will be served in strawberry, chocolate, and vanilla-flavored cups," Vijaya said. Presently (June 2023), they are selling 100 ml. cups with 90 ml. filling capacity. "We will soon upgrade them to 120 ml. cups to meet the market demand". The cups are in great demand in Karnataka, Kerala, T.N., Dubai and Saudi Arabia. *Hip. . .Hip. . Hurrah to the Start-Uppers!* (The Hindu, 16.06.2023)

> ***"Plastic pollution-free world is not a choice; it's a commitment to the next generation.*** (Amit Ray)
> ******

Tuber-based Rainbow Diet

The Central Tuber Crops Research Institute (CTCRI), TVPM - a constituent institute of the Indian Council of Agricultural Research (ICAR) based in TVPM - launched a campaign in Aattpadi in Palakkad where it show-cased a tuber-based rainbow diet with bio-fortified sweet potato, cassava and millets. It is a meal plan with different colored fresh fruits and vegetables. The colors in these natural foods are due to specific phytonutrients. "It's so named because besides being healthy, it also brightens up the food plate with rainbow colors," so says the scientists. ICAR will launch the diet in Odisha in the current financial year (2023-2024) and plans to cover nine districts in the State by the end of 2024-2025. The CTCRI is gearing up to give wide publicity to this special item in areas with sizable tribal populations to tackle malnutrition and ensure a balanced diet. "In Odisha, the campaign will be launched in nine districts," said P.S. Sivakumar, the project leader. In 2020, the institute introduced bio-fortified sweet potatoes in certain districts in Arunachal Pradesh and Tripura. With the tuber-based rainbow diet, the institute is popularizing orange-fleshed and purple-fleshed sweet potato and purple-fleshed yam. *What more to expect from ICAR & CTCRI?* (The Hindu, 20.06.2023)

Endnote:

"The evermore sophisticated weapons piling up in the arsenals of the wealthiest and of the mightiest can kill the illiterate, the ill, the poor and the hungry, but they cannot kill ignorance, illness, poverty or hunger." (Fidel Castro) Every gun that is made, every warship launched, every rocket fired, signifies in the final sense a theft from those who hunger and are not fed, those who are cold and are not clothed." (D. D. Eisenhower) It is said that one-third of humanity goes to bed hungry every night and many children still die of hunger, not because Mother Earth has failed to produce enough for her children. The enemies that lurk behind hunger and starvation are selfishness, apathy, and the non-caring attitude of those who have more than enough. We don't need to be rich to feed the hungry; we need to have eyes to see, ears to hear and a heart to care enough.

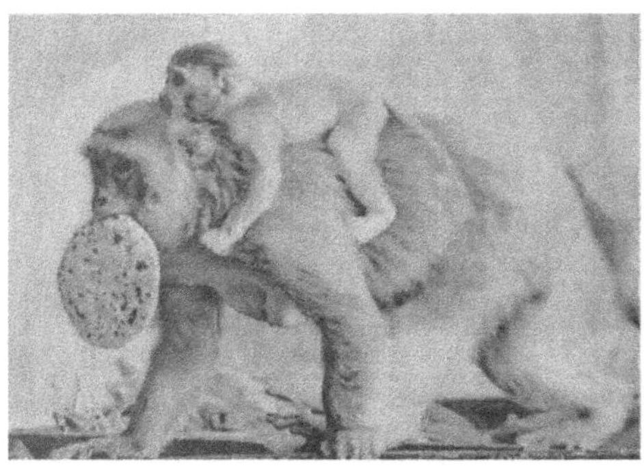

III
ON THE LADDER OF LITERACY & LEARNING

International Literacy Day (ILD) is celebrated every year on 08 September to make everyone aware of the meaning and importance of literacy for individuals and societies. Literacy is the ability to read, write, speak and listen in such a way that it helps us to understand what is read or heard and communicate effectively. A person with no passion for reading is just like a little baby with no passion for breastfeeding. As our life-sustaining oxygen is found in clean air, life-prospering knowledge is found in good books. Writing and reading bind together people of distant epochs and the distance in time and space is reduced. Good books are lighthouses giving a sense of direction to globe-trotters as well as knowledge-trotters. "To read is to fly; it is to soar to the point of vantage which gives a view over wide terrains of history, human variety, ideas, shared experience and the fruits of many inquiries."(A.C. Grayling)

In literacy, Kerala stands first among the Indian States and is the only State in India where over 94% of the people can read and write. To spread the message of literacy and education and thereby make life bloom, blossom and fructify to its full potential, much needs to be done along the breadth and length of India. Here are a few inspiring examples of some committed individuals and groups who have taken upon themselves the mission of spreading the message of Education for a Better Tomorrow among the last and the least who live in the periphery, unaware of what happens outside their by-lanes and to convince them that "there is another sky, ever serene and fair."

******

Out of the Box, Under the Bridge

Rajesh Kumar Sharma's school has no desks and no chairs. The roof of the school is a metro railway bridge 10 meters overhead. The blackboards are rectangles painted on the wall of the adjacent station. Despite its makeshift nature, the school offers hope to a few impoverished children in the neighborhood. The idea to open this special school dawned upon Rajesh (41) during a morning walk when he saw some children weeding and picking flowers. "I asked them which school they go to, and they looked at me in wonder and did not answer," Rajesh said. "It had not occurred to me before that not every child has access to a school."

Rajesh, who runs a grocery across the street from the Yamuna Vihar Metro Station, started this special school in 2006 to offer free basic education to the children of the local laborers and farmers. Together with his friend Laxmi Chandra, a retired teacher, Rajesh started classes under the metro bridge for two hours in the morning on weekdays. After the government enacted the Right to Education Act (2009), which guarantees free schooling for children between the ages of 06 and 14, Rajesh focused on preparing the children for admission to school and helping them cope with the curriculum. As trains rumble overhead and traffic rolls past a few meters away, the students who number more than 70, sit on foam mats and recite after their teachers, numbers and alphabets or what has been taught previously. They are taught the English alphabet, mathematics, multiplication tables, geometry, history and more. "These are children who cannot afford private tuition to help them with their school homework," Chandra said. "We teach them in a way no one cares to."

Rajesh initially bore the entire cost of providing the children with textbooks, pencils and exercise books. Later, people who heard about the school began dropping off supplies, sometimes anonymously. "One man came with 60 school bags once," Rajesh said. "He would not tell me his name or other details about himself. He said none of that mattered as long as the children got a decent education." Rajesh has to battle constantly to get parents to send their children to his classes for a couple of hours each day. All it takes to enroll in government schools, which also provide free lunch, is for a parent to accompany the child to register their name. Most parents of the children whom Rajesh teaches are reluctant to do even that. Being squatters, they have no residency papers and are loath to interact with the authorities, fearing that it might draw attention to their illegally constructed huts.

At 13, Kunti Kumari is one of the oldest girls studying the alphabet at Rajesh's school. She joined the school but discontinued after a month. On visiting her house, Rajesh understood her situation. Kunti works alongside her parents in the fields. After the euphoria of her first month of learning wore off, she struggled to keep up with the burden of working and studying. She wakes up at 03 am every day to cut roses from the family's bushes for her father to take them to the market by 06 am. She then helps her younger sister Babli (11) with household chores before setting off to attend her class. After she returns home and completes her share of work in the fields, she is often too tired to do homework. "The parents don't understand," Rajesh said. It was only after he made Kunti recite the alphabet from A is for Apple all the way to S is for Ship that her father was convinced that the two hours of daily schooling were worth it. Kunti and her sister both attend Rajesh's school now, taking their two young brothers along instead of having to stay at home to babysit them while their parents are at work. But their father has not yet enrolled them in a government school. "They don't understand the system," Kunti said. "I wish I could say outright I want to go to school, but I know I must help my parents support our family." *Hai Rajesh, you are a Raja in the hearts and minds of your children.* (sbhattacharya@thenational.ae, Suryatapa Bhattacharya, 15. 04. 2013)

"Education breeds confidence. Confidence breeds hope. Hope breeds peace." (Confucius)

******

They Reach Out to Village Children

It all began in 2002 when a few young men in their 20s got connected to online groups to promote local music, art and theater. After working unofficially for a few years, they formed *Aviratha* (Ceaseless, Uninterrupted), a Comprehensive School Development Programme (CSDP) for the tribal children in Chamarajanagar, covering 11 schools. Working from a tiny room in Jayanagar, Satheesh, Himanshu and the team are driven by a common desire to contribute towards building a better society and to ensure that the penniless also get equal access to food, education, housing etc. "Unequal access to education hinders upward social movement. Everyone should have access to the same resources," said Satheesh, a software engineer. CSDP now has 25 core members and 120 volunteers aged between 20 and 70 from different walks of life. It has no single donor but runs on donations from like-minded people.

The turning point came in 2009 when they raised Rs.10,00,000/- in 10 days for relief work in the flood-hit villages in Koppal and Dharwad. "We provided the victims with food, clothes, medicines, drinking water and conducted health camps," said Himanshu, Asst. Prof. at the Rajiv Gandhi Institute for Public Health and Centre for Disease Control, Bengaluru. Once people saw the proper utilization of their money, they wanted to get involved. Buoyant by the response, CSDP decided to rebuild a partially destroyed Lower Primary School in Shaliganur village of Gangavathi Taluk in Koppal. An architect was hired and the school was rebuilt in a year using eco-friendly material to ensure that it is compatible with the weather. The govt. joined hands by constructing the compound walls and toilets.

In 2009, CSDP started the Note Books Distribution drive in 22 schools in Dodda Aladha Mara outside the city. "We want to have effective long-term programs, not merely touch-and-go measures. With our unique and sustainable programs, we want to help the underprivileged to our maximum capacity," said Himanshu. Along with Sakhi Trust, a Hospet-based NGO, the team looks forward to the higher education of girls who have finished SSLC. Almost 80 girls are set to benefit under the program that rolled out in August 2016. (ToI, 18.09.2016)

*"Education is the key to unlocking the world.
It is the passport to freedom."* (O. Winfrey)
******

Visually Impaired, Mentally Enlightened

Deepa secured 92% marks in the SSLC exam conducted in 2017. It is a great achievement for Deepa, a visually impaired student of Ambubai Residential School for Blind Girls. She spent a considerable amount of time after school at Mitra Jyothi (Friends of Light), a foundation in HSR Layout, Bengaluru, that assists the visually impaired and prepared herself to meet the challenges of the exam with the help of audio and Braille books available at the center.

Established in 1990, Mitra Jyothi (MJ) is a registered Trust that has been behind many success stories. Madhu Shinghal, the Founder and Managing Trustee of MJ, lives and works and challenges her impaired vision. "The visually impaired individuals should be respected and looked upon as equals. We want to bring in this equality. Their challenge heightens once they go for higher education. There isn't much help available. We are working towards providing them with materials and other resources," said Madhu. The Education Resource Centre of the Trust supports the education of those destitute of vision. It provides accessible reading materials and runs a digital talking book library with over 2654 books recorded and edited by volunteers. The students can access them by paying Rs.15/- per CD. They also have a monthly audio magazine called Sanchaya and have recorded books for Civil Service aspirants.

Independent Living Skills is the most fundamental hands-on program of MJ that enables persons with visual disabilities to be trained in skills such as cooking, tailoring and other life skills needed for self-reliant living. The Computer Training Centre imparts basic and advanced computer literacy. The Placement Cell provides job placement assistance to those with various disabilities and many former students who are serving in reputed companies.

"Until I was told about Mitra Jyothi, I felt I would never get a job. I was groomed for my interview here," said Megana K.I., working with Computer Information System Company (CISCO). MJ has a center in Electronic City, Bengaluru, for the Empowerment of Women with disabilities. The much-talked-about technology-driven society of today needs to have a conducive environment and create awareness in the minds of all, for the true inclusivity of those with disabilities, in mainstream society. (The Hindu, 16.06.2017)

"Being challenged in life is inevitable
Being defeated is optional." (R. Crawford)

******

Bhuvaneswari Won the Battle

Child marriages among tribal communities are not rare events. It has been reported that due to the timely intervention of enlightened citizens and govt. authorities, between 2014 and 2017, a total of about 550 child marriages were prevented in tribal and rural areas of Visakhapatnam, Vizianagaram and Srikakulam. Here's our heroine, Kodingi Bhuvaneswari of Champi near Araku in Andhra Pradesh, who turned her personal story into a telling message for teenage girls, their parents and society at large. As she turned 17, her parents decided that it was time that she discontinued her studies, tied the knot and lived in the shadow of her husband and in-laws. But Bhuvaneswari had a different vision of life and decided to live up to her name, Bhuvaneswari, which means Goddess of the world. Clearly and boldly, she told her parents that she wanted to continue her education, be employed and be financially independent. Her parents initially demurred and locked her up at home, citing the example of her two elder sisters who were married off at a tender age. Faced with the iron determination of the girl, the parents relented and Bhuvaneswari from the Bhagata tribe passed her Intermediate course with 71.1% marks from A.S. Raja Women's College in Visakhapatnam. Later, she passed an online Teacher Training Course run by the State Government. "I had to gather a lot of courage to stand alone in my fight," she told The Hindu. Her rebellion against early marriage and her decision to pursue education has made her a role model for the growing generation of girls. In her counseling sessions, she challenges the girls to follow their inner voice and pursue education and not to fall into the trap set by a generation that looked upon girls as fit only for the kitchen and bedroom. *Well Done, Great Lady Bhuvaneswari! Congratulations!!* (The Hindu, 21.06.2017)

To achieve success:
Plan Purposefully, Prepare Prayerfully,
Proceed Positively, Pursue Persistently.
******

A Library on Wheels

"A library is a temple of learning and learning has liberated more people than all the wars in history." (C.T. Rowan) Bengaluru is famous as a city of many internationally acclaimed temples of learning. However, not many know about a temple of learning that moves on wheels, fittingly named *Njana Vahini* (Carrier of Knowledge) and lives up to its name. Loaded with knowledge in the form of good books, it travels to five govt. schools in South Bengaluru every Saturday. On a weekly basis, this mobile library offers about 700 books to the children. Started by young working professionals in their mid-20s and 30s, the library on wheels aims to instill the habit of reading among the growing generation. Books ranging from general knowledge to comics, novels, encyclopedias, and biographies of great personalities are available in Kannada and English, "I saw the immense potential in kids when I worked as a substitute teacher in a government. school. So when one of my friends gave me a four-wheeler, I decided to use it for a mobile library," said Aman Jain, the Founder-President of Zav Foundation that runs the library. Students of class VI to VIII in govt. schools at Ittamadu, Arehalli, Chikkalasandra and Hoskerahalli are issued borrowers' cards. They can keep the books for a week. "Catering to about 3,500 students, we have issued 25-30 cards to each school," Mr. Jain said. (The Hindu, 16.06.2017)

*"**Keep Reading. It is one of the most marvelous adventures that anyone can have**". (Lloyd Alexander)*

******

BookMobile - Let's Read India

With the umpteen streaming services, apps and other internet platforms available to most readers, many have moved away from the pleasure of holding a good book in hand, sitting on a comfortable chair in the open verandah or under a shady tree and reading to their heart's content. While urban dwellers with easy accessibility to digital resources often take reading for granted, the reality is poles apart for those in interior regions. Putting his finger on the need for the reading habit to be reinstated, especially in non-urban settings, Prafulla Wankhede, along with his team of nine, inaugurated in September 2020 a mobile library initiative named Let's Read India.

"Many times, I have traveled to Europe for work, where I saw a few mobile library initiatives. Drawing inspiration from it, I formed a team about two years ago, and with a GPS management system, we decided to get the project rolling while keeping in mind the demographic particularities of different areas and what they like to read," says Wankhede. Borrowing a book from the traveling library comes with one condition - the borrower, no matter what his/her age, must submit a 300-360 word review of the book after reading it. Only then the reader is permitted to pick up another one. Through this review system, by the time the book reaches the tenth person, because of the previous reviews, that person can determine whether he/she would actually like to read the book or not. The reviews can be written on paper or submitted online through their website or on Twitter.

"Most books in libraries catch dust, so we felt, why not have such libraries that bring books to the people to encourage them to get into the habit of reading. This system helped us gauge the type of books readers tend to gravitate to. We have a young reader who has been routinely borrowing from us for the past eight months and I feel he might've exhausted the science-related section. It's a joy for us to see these kids sit down, read and learn. It's brought about a lot of positivity in my life as well," Wankhede adds. The mobile library covers around 20 to 60 km. a day and those who wish to donate books to the library can get in touch with the librarians by calling the office, visiting the website or dropping them a tweet.

The group has plans to expand its initiative across the country. "We do have plans of moving to other places as well but the lockdown has made it a tad difficult to navigate. For now, we're bound to Navi Mumbai, Raigad and a few other parts of Maharashtra. We hope to start a YouTube channel to educate people on this as well", Wankhede signs off. (gayathri.chandran@mid-day.com, 12.04.2021)

Naidu Adopted 70 Children on 70th I–Day

Parvathareddi Parthasaradhi Naidu, a Chittoor-based social worker, looks beyond distributing uniforms and books to school children; he wants them to imbibe patriotism and grow up into citizens committed to nation building. For four decades, Naidu (76), a household name in Chittoor, Andhra Pradesh, has been extending financial and moral support to hundreds of families affected by poverty and life-threatening ailments. When Mother India celebrated her Sapthathi (70 years) as a free nation, Naidu adopted 70 children from the local Municipal School and an Anganwadi center of Balaji Nagar. Naidu said that by adopting the school children mostly belonging to urban poor households, he did not merely mean the distribution of books and uniforms, stationery and food. "At this age, I look at them as vibrant builders of the country's destiny. Apart from their regular welfare, I wish the young minds to learn the true meaning of Independence Day Celebrations and imbibe the spirit of patriotism," he said.

The veteran social worker said that in the last decade, he had been pursuing the dream of bringing the school kids to the libraries. He wanted to devote his time to helping them study and understand the lives of great leaders who brought freedom to our country. "This will make the new-gen patriotically strong citizens," he added. Naidu arranges regular moral lessons for the growing generation and helps them to participate in cultural activities and physical fitness training. The school authorities and parents are all praise for Naidu's gesture towards the future citizens of India. (The Hindu 15.08.2017)

"Education is what remains after one has forgotten what one has learnt in school."
(Albert Einstein)
******

UP. . UP. . UP. . in the Sky

For the special children from the Special Schools functioning under *Sarvasiksha Abhyan,* Thripunithura Block Resource Centre, it was a day ever to be cherished and never to be forgotten. Till 11 September 2017, they had only seen airplanes up in the sky and had discussed among themselves how nice it would be to fly like that up in the air. Their wish and dream became a reality when on the morning of 12 September 2017, an IndiGo plane rose majestically from Cochin International Airport Ltd. (CIAL) carrying 50 special children studying in Std II to Std VII, accompanied by 17 teachers and a doctor. As they climbed the steps to the plane, holding tight to their teachers' hands, they had no idea what was in store for them.

As the man-made winged bird took off, momentarily, they were scared and tightened their grip on the supportive hands of their teachers. Then it was smiles, clapping of hands, Hip. . . Hip. . . Hurrah!!!. . .How great!! and more exclamations!!!. After an hour, they were brought down from their dreamy world at TVPM Airport. Our special future citizens were a bit sad since Shri Pinarayi Vijayan, the CM, was not there to receive them. Instead, Dr. T.N. Seema, Vice Chairperson of Haritha Kerala Mission and G.S. Pradeep of Aswamedham fame accorded them a warm welcome. They visited the Secretariat, Legislative Assembly Hall, Zoo and more. By 4.30 pm, they were comfortably seated in a bus that carried them back to their homes. It is left to the imagination of the reader how they talked endlessly, excitedly describing their experience to their parents, siblings and classmates.

This special flight was sponsored by Arakkathazhath Luis, a Non-Resident Keralite (NRK) who runs the Sunrise Fitness Centre at Udayamperoor, Thripoonithura. During one of his visits to the Special School, he asked the children if they wished for anything and the answer was: *Vimana-yathra* (Airplane flight). Luis promised them a Vimana-yathra then and kept his word later. (Deepika, 13.09.2017)

*"Never doubt that a few thoughtful &
committed citizens can change the world.
Indeed, it's the only thing that ever has."* (M. Mead)

******

Girija Teacher's Love-Laden Gift

When needs like infrastructure development, playgrounds, the extension of buildings etc., arise, it is customary for institutions to ask for sponsors, knowing well that there are generous people who extend a helping hand willingly to such noble causes. When Ms. Girija, HM of Govt. Vocational Higher Secondary School, Thirumaradi, saw the children of private schools having umpteen facilities to enjoy their playtime, she was saddened by the fact that the children in her school did not have these facilities. Then, the idea of creating a Kid's Park for the school sparked in her motherly heart. The proposal was welcomed wholeheartedly by the PTA of the school. But she did not waste time drafting appealing appeals to nudge the well-wishers and would-be sponsors to contribute generously. Instead, from her own pocket, she spent Rs.1,50,000/- to make a Kids' Park for the juvenile generation of her school. She spent her hard-earned money to clear the ground, plant a garden and install play items like a merry-go-round, swings, horse see-saw, funnel ball game and more.

Girija teacher's dream park was inaugurated in August 2017. When Girija, the children-centered teacher, sees the children enjoying their free time in the park, singing and swinging, laughing and giggling, shouting and fighting, going round and round on the merry-go-round, her maternal heart beats happily. The PTA has promised to install more play items in the newborn park. *Girija means born on the mountain. Our HM Girija carries a mountain of love in her heart!* (Manorama 18,08.2017)

"You have not lived today until you have done something for someone who can never repay you." (John Bunyan)
******

They Happily Cycle to School

As many as 400 flood-hit students in Alappuzha Dt. have been provided cycles under the I am for Alleppey campaign launched by Alappuzha District Administration in September 2018, to help rebuild the 2018 flood-hit district. Since then, it has launched an array of initiatives. Many people have joined the campaign by donating money for rebuilding damaged hospitals, Anganwadis and other public institutions in the district. Besides, it has distributed cattle to dairy farmers, boats to fishermen and so on. The campaign has undertaken the construction of 500 disaster-resilient houses for the flood-affected people in the district. (The Hindu. 08.09.2019)

(Chinese Proverb)
******

Maruti Alto's Rebirth as Library Alto

It is not yet time to forget the torturous shut-down days inflicted on humanity by the treacherous COVID-19, the unending smoke and smell from cremation grounds attacking the nostrils of passers-by and hundreds of bodies lined up, with their relatives keeping guard over them and waiting to move the bodies to be cremated and be done with it. Dr Biju Balakrishnan (41), a professor of the Sree Krishna College, Guruvayoor, Thrissur Dt. was not in his home town Karakonam, TVPM, around 320 km. south of Thrissur when the lockdown was announced. As soon as he returned from Guruvayoor, Biju enrolled himself as a COVID-19 volunteer and worked with government agencies to spread the message of social distancing and other precautions against the spread of the pandemic. "The idea of a mobile library struck me when I thought of helping some students in the neighborhood who could not visit my home library owing to lockdown restrictions," Biju said.

The response to the idea of a mobile library was so encouraging that he decided to extend the service to more people and posted a brief message with his contact number on social media. It went viral, and he started receiving calls from other panchayats as well. He converted his Maruti Alto car into a mobile library. "I distribute textbooks for school and college students, novels, science fiction, classics and works of other genres. They are all from my personal library, which has more than 6,000 books," Biju said. He has also distributed books among homemakers, senior citizens, police personnel and medical workers. He leaves the house every day with a stack of 300 books and parks his car at a random locality and lends books to residents there. "The aim is to help the less privileged, those who would never have visited a library," he said. Ever since he began his mission on 05 April 2020, Biju has distributed around 2,850 books to people across seven panchayats under the Parasala Assembly Constituency.

Biju, a poet and a regular contributor to local newspapers and magazines says: "The reading culture is so strong here that it was one of the first things people missed when the lockdown began." He aims to reach out to as many reading enthusiasts as possible who are currently missing out on reading, as libraries have been shut because of the lockdown. While it is true that several publishing houses are offering free e-books to overcome boredom during the lockdown, Biju says that the feel of a real book cannot possibly be replicated. "I mostly operate through my phone and drive around 30 km. on an average daily, to reach out to readers. Before I approach a certain panchayat, I inform the locals who are interested in reading to come to a designated place and collect the books. A good number of the borrowers are students and middle-aged. The youth seem to be addicted to their phones," he said. Anyone can pick any book from the boot of his car. When does he intend to collect the books back? "Some have returned them after reading, while others haven't. Many may have passed the books on to others to read, I hope," he says. Admittedly, he is not expecting the bulk of his books to be returned. "It doesn't matter, really. As long as they are read, I am happy," he adds. He is also the coordinator of *Sooryakanthi* and *Akshara-madhuram*, two educational projects run by C K Hareendran, MLA. A former research officer with the State Institute of Languages, Biju has published three books. (Readers Digest India, 17.04.2020, TNIE, 24.04 2020)

"Let's be reasonable and add an eighth day to the week that is devoted exclusively to reading." (Lena Dunham)

******

Daya Loves Children and Books

"Children should grow up reading. Their home should become a library. Classrooms and homes should be filled with books," says Daya (= Mercy), a caring teacher with an eye to the future. But she doesn't stop just talking about books and reading. She makes sure that children get books at home that suit their age and intelligence. Deprived of regular school, friends and outdoor games, children were the worst hit during the COVID-19 lockdown. Daya, a teacher at Sree Ramakrishna Gurukula Vidyamandir LP School, Thrissur, took innovative steps to engage her budding scholars positively and gainfully during those worrying days. With the active support of publishers and well-wishers, in the academic year 2020-2021, Daya organized books for 42 children in Class III B, who were mostly from Adattu Grama Panchayat. The students were asked to collect books from neighbors and relatives. To this, she added books from her home library too. She asked parents to present books to their children as birthday gifts instead of dresses and ice cream. There are 10 to 100 books in the personal libraries of every student now. When the school reopened on 01 June 2021, her student Diya gave a surprise gift to her teacher Daya by reciting one of the poems from *Pularithuval*, which is Poet P.K. Gopi's book for children. (The Hindu, 12.06.2021)

"Today a Reader, Tomorrow a Leader." (M. Fuller)
******

Thayammal is Real Amma

Thayammal, who has studied only up to Class IV, knows no high-sounding quotes about the need for educating the growing generation to secure a happy future for themselves and for the society in which they live and move and have their being. A tender coconut seller Thayammal's magnanimous contribution of Rs.1,00,000/- to upgrade the infrastructure of a Panchayat School in Tiruppur, Tamil Nadu, was cited by PM Narendra Modi in his Mann Ki Baat address to the nation to highlight how awareness of education is visible at every level of society. Modiji said: "Thayammalji, from Udumalpet Block of Tiruppur District of Tamil Nadu, is a very inspiring person. For years, her family has been making a living by selling tender coconuts. Her financial condition leaves much to be desired, but she leaves no stone unturned to educate her son and daughter who are studying in Chinnaveerampatti Panchayat School." Modi added that he was overwhelmed by Thayammal's sense of social responsibility and her contribution of Rs.1,00,000/- to upgrade her village school. Surprised that the PM referred to her, Thayammal said, "I never expected the PM to mention my name. When I took my daughter to the COVID-19 vaccination camp in the school, I heard the staff discussing the urgent infrastructure needs of the school. I talked it over to my husband Arumugam and we donated Rs.1,00,000/- which we saved by selling tender coconuts. I was surprised that this caught the media and the country's top leader's attention."

Born in Kottampatti village near Pollachi, Thayammal could study only till Class IV, but she was aware of the importance of education. She has put to shame the so-called rich and powerful of the land who splurge money on lavish weddings, foreign trips and festive gatherings but are reluctant to contribute towards any developmental program. Dear Thayammal, your love for education comes not from books but from your commitment to familial and societal well-being. We are proud of you! (Mathrubhoomi, 03.02.2022; Wikipedia)

"A single act of kindness throws out roots in all directions, and the roots spring up and make new trees."
******

The Sarojini Damodaran Foundation

Amid the dark clouds gifted by the rogue virus, some people with helping hands and giving hearts painted a few silver linings which boosted the suffering humanity to hold on to their hope and keep muttering: The best is yet to be. There was an unprecedented, uplifting display of solidarity and ordinary human's inclination to be kind and helpful that took various routes like the supply of food, medicine, scholarships for financially backward students and more. To this category can be added the Sarojini Damodaran Foundation (SDF) established by Kumari Shibulal and SD Shibulal (Co-founder & Former CEO, Infosys), with their scholarship schemes to ignite a spark in the minds of the youngsters and to inspire them to achieve their full potential. Apart from educational scholarships, the SDF contributes towards healthcare, organic farming, nutrition and social welfare across India.

On 10 March 2023, Mathrubhoomi reported that the SDF has taken up the education of 134 children in Alappuzha District who were orphaned during the COVID-19's reign of terror. The project will function under the We Are for Alleppey scheme earlier inaugurated by V.R. Krishna Teja, the much-loved Collector of Alappuzha. The complete expenses of the education of these children till they pass Std. XII will be met by the SDF. After Plus Two, those who get a seat in the merit quota of any professional course will get the needed financial help from the Foundation. Hip. . .Hip. . .Hurrah! Long Live SDF! (Mathrubhoomi, 10.03.2023)

"The happiest are those who do the most for others."
(B.T. Washington)
******

Teja Brought Thejas to Their Lives

In January 2021, Siya (name changed) lost her father, the only breadwinner of the family, to

COVID-19. Siya, who always cherished the dream of serving the suffering humanity as a nurse, studied hard and obtained 92% marks in the Plus Two exam a year later. But where is the money to pursue her dream? She found the answer in the *We Are for Alleppey* initiative spearheaded by the then District Collector V.R. Krishna Teja. "The Collector found me a sponsor to bear the total expenses of my education and helped me to enroll myself at St. Thomas Nursing College, Kattanam," says Siya.

The project *We Are for Alleppey* ensures comprehensive care and protection to 293 children who lost both parents to the pandemic, the majority of them from impoverished backgrounds, to continue their education with the support of sponsors. It also takes care of their health, housing and other needs. Some of them pursuing undergraduate studies were forced to discontinue their academic pursuits and take up odd jobs to meet the basic needs of their family. The project has brought them back to their classrooms and books. "It is the best example of how film stars and corporate companies, teachers and doctors, politicians and industrialists, et al. can form a single platform and work together for a good cause. Most of the sponsors have promised to provide assistance to these children throughout their years of study," Teja says. Among the beneficiaries are 73 students pursuing graduation, 37 Plus Two, 65 High School, 41 Upper Primary and 17 Lower Primary. *We Are for Alleppey*, with the Collector as patron, has been registered as a Society. (The Hindu, 18.03.2023)

"The strength of the team is each individual member. The strength of each member is the team." (P. Jackson)

******

A Library for Tribal Kids

A room crammed with hundreds of books for sale? No, they are not literary works of famous writers or world-class journals but old textbooks and other study materials. The Bapuji Smaraka Vayanasala at Perumkulam in Kollam has been collecting textbooks for distribution among tribal students across the State, studying in classes IX-XII. "While all the students from Class I to VIII get free textbooks, most tribal students in higher classes skip textbook purchase as their families cannot afford it, "said the Principal of HSS, Kisumam, Pathanamthitta Dt. "When I joined there last October, none of the tribal students had textbooks even months into the academic year . . . So the library started the initiative to make books available to them," says V. Vijesh, Secretary of the library. So far, the library has received over 5,000 books, even as heavy packages continue to arrive and will continue till the end of May 2023. Then, these books will be sorted out and sent to those districts with high tribal populations, such as Wayanad, Idukki and Palakkad. P.S. Sreekumari, HM of Government U.P. School, Pennukara, Alappuzha, has collected about 500 books from her former students. "Many of us had no idea that the students in tribal areas have been managing without textbooks. When I told my students about the initiative, they started bringing in textbooks, notebooks and guides," says Sreekumari. The students are contacted through various social networking platforms. "We have a contact person in every district that collects the books and despatches them to us," says Vijesh. Though they started collecting books immediately after the final exams in 2023, the fear is that in June 2023, when the school reopens, the demand will be more than the books available for distribution. After the reopening, the listed schools will be contacted for the exact number of books required and the books will be delivered to them within two weeks," says Vijesh. (The Hindu, 20.05.2023)

"Education is a better safeguard of liberty than a standing army." (E. Everett)

******

NGOs are Stellar Contributors

India has made steady and sturdy progress in primary and secondary education after 1947. However, there are many stumbling blocks on Mother India's climb on the ladder of universal literacy and learning. Nevertheless, it is encouraging to note that several non-governmental, non-profit organizations in the country have been filling the gaps in education. Here are a few NGOs (placed in chronological order) that are bent on fighting the titanic forces of class-caste divisions and gender-based indiscretions and place India in an enviable position on the education map of the world.

Trivandrum Don Bosco Veedu Society

Don Bosco Veedu is a registered Society that caters to the welfare of underprivileged children and youth and those on the periphery of society, impacting meaningful changes in their lives and seeking to empower them with the skills they need to effect changes in their lives and within their communities. The Vision of the Society is to create child-friendly communities by collectively working as catalysts to transform adults to think and act in favor of children, especially those at risk. From the above Vision follows the Mission to reach out and rescue children and youth at risk due to illiteracy, drugs, alcohol, sexual abuse etc., and to inspire them to walk out of such situations and work towards a dignified life that would result in a woman and child friendly society. It was started without much fanfare in May 1991, with a night shelter for street children and youth in a rented facility at Bishop Pereira Hall, Shankumugham, TVPM. Later, the shelter home was shifted to Manacaud with the name Don Bosco Veedu. The Society runs the following projects for the welfare of women and children: 1. Childline focuses on children in any basic need and ensures their rights and protection. 2. Open Shelter Home for Children and Youth at Risk. 3. Drug Rehabilitation Education for Children. 4. Karimadom Education & Empowerment Network (KEEN). 5. Kerala Interstate Migrants' Alliance for Transformation (KISMAT), a project for the care and restoration of the rights of the interstate migrant population. The Society is registered as a non-profit, charitable society under the Travancore-Cochin Literary, Scientific and Charitable Societies Registration Act, 1955 (965/91). Over the years, the Foundation has impacted many families and continues to do so. (www.dbveedu.org)

"Home is the starting place of love, hope and dreams."

******

Alleppey Diocesan Social Welfare Society

The Society is registered under The Travancore-Cochin Literary, Scientific, and Charitable Social Welfare Society, Alleppey Diocese, Registration Act XII of 1955. S. No. A 141/78 of 1978. (locally known as Alleppey Diocesan Society (ADS). The Vision of the society speaks of the integral development of the entire population in the coastal territories of Alleppey and Ernakulam Districts of the State of Kerala in India, while the Mission is to empower the target population to self-reliance through developmental activities. Below are the activities undertaken to achieve the above goals.

Activities:
Save a Family Plan helps around 300 families to become financially self-reliant.

Kolping India, which is affiliated with Kolping International, named after Adolph Kolping (1813-1865), a German priest, and works towards the holistic development of the marginalized communities in the area.

Catholic Health Association of India provides help towards a better quality of life for 152 differently-abled children.

Navajeevan-Disaster Risk Reduction, affiliated to Caritas India - Caritas Germany. Disaster Clinics are constituted in a dozen places along the

Alappuzha coasts which undertake the formation and training of village-level task forces.

Ashakiranam Cancer Care Campaign aims at better awareness of cancer and its prevention and brings solace and support to those under the attack of the killer disease.

Childline Alappuzha, a Central Govt. project functions to prevent physical, emotional, and sexual abuse of children and provide assistance to those in need. Its special mission is to make child marriage, child labor, child beggary etc., things of the past.

Kaval a State Govt. project provides psycho-social care for Children in Conflict with the Law (CCL).

Precious Children's Programme extends financial support to brilliant students from financially backward families.

The Nurture Project targets coastal areas of the diocese. "Nurture nature and nature will nurture us" is the theme of the project.

Currently (2023), a total of 1900 families are helped through the above projects, some of which are financially supported by certain foreign agencies. (adsalleppey@gmail.com)

"I cannot do all the good that the world needs.
But the world needs all the good that I can do." (J.Stanfield)

******

Aarti Home for Girls

In 1992, a washerwoman approached Sandhya Puchalapalli, a Govt. School teacher with a two-year-old Radhika, whose father had killed her mother and Radhika was abandoned on the streets of Kadappa, AP. Sandhya decided to be the foster mother of the thrown-out child, and that was a deciding moment in her life. Together with a few kind-hearted colleagues, she established a home for a few deserted girls and that was the beginning of Aarti Home for Girls, an orphanage for abandoned and destitute girls. Here, orphaned girls are provided with love and care, shelter and security, education and opportunities to make a mark in life in a less institutionalized and family-based environment. Over 650 children from disadvantaged backgrounds are currently enrolled in Aarti School. It runs a helpline center and also serves as a center for livelihood training. (www.aartiforgirls.org).

"Are not there heights that a girl can reach given the chance? Intelligence knows no sex."

******

K.C. Mahindra Education Trust & Nanhi Kali

Anand Mahindra, Chairman of Mahindra Group, began Project Nanhi Kali (Little Bud) in 1996 with the objective of educating the underprivileged girl children of Mother India. Since its inception, this flagship program that enables marginalized girls to complete 10 years of schooling has helped over 4.5 lakh girls. Its focus is on decreasing the school drop-out rates and ensuring that girl children from socially and economically backward families get quality education. Those interested in the education of the poor can participate in the program and sponsor the education of one (or more) underprivileged girl child for a minimum period of one year. (www.nanhikali.org)

"I have courage, I am bold. Do not try to keep me in hold.
Let me grow up and I will hold you up."

******

Ibtada

Ibtada (Beginning in Urdu) is a non-profit, non-governmental development organization headquartered in Alwar, functioning in the Mewat region of Rajasthan. Started in 1997, Ibtada's mission is to work for women and girl children and in the last 25 years, it has reached out to hundreds of households in 400 plus villages of 6 blocks in Alwar District. The core of Ibtada's mission is to promote community-based institutions such as Self-Help Groups (SHG), Clusters and Federations (Manch), which form the base for implementing different programs for financial inclusion, livelihoods, girls' empowerment and rights and entitlements. These institutions help women to change power relations in their homes and in society, foster decision-making abilities, enhance their control over family finances and provide them space for visibility and collective action. Currently, four federations - Chetna, Kranti, Sangharsh, and Savera (Life, Revolution, Battle, Morning) registered as Trusts, work autonomously with the support of Ibtada to bring the deprived women of this region to the mainstream by educating and empowering them through literacy, life skills, computer know-how and vocational training. It also provides financial support to improve infrastructure in the government. schools. (www.ibtada.in)

"Education is everything. Education is your power.
Education is your way in life for whatever you want to do."
******

Adarsh Charitable Trust

Established in 1998, Adarsh Charitable Trust (ACT) is a registered non-profit NGO that started as a Day Care Centre with seven differently-abled children. With early sensory-motor developmental therapy and academic training, it has many success stories to its credit. In the last 25 years, around 86 students left Adarsh with their disability factor considerably reduced and confidence and social interaction ability levels built up to pursue their studies in mainstream schools. It is an accepted fact that in the matter of rehabilitation, the earlier the intervention, the better. Hence, a very welcome feature in the growth pattern of Adarsh is the increased enrolment of young children below 6 years every year. Out of around 300 children at its two main rehabilitation centers, around 30 of them constitute an Early Intervention Group. Presently, it enjoys the status of a Prestigious Centre of Excellence in the coaching and rehabilitation of youngsters with special needs. Adarsh has hired vans, which pick up children from within a radius of about 30-40 km. and drop them back at their homes at the end of the school session. Undoubtedly this is a great facility; it is a great blessing to the children with special care and to their parents. (www.adarshrehab.org)

Vidya and Child

Established in 1998, this NGO works in marginalized communities, exploring the unique potential of each child by providing opportunities for value-integrated learning and development. It aims at making a difference in the lives of the underprivileged children belonging to penurious sections of society, the majority of whom are first-generation learners whose parents work as domestic servants, rickshaw pullers, industrial workers, plumbers, street vendors and so on. Over 1800 children from Nursery to Class XII and after, in semi-rural and rural settings, are being helped through school and after-school-support programs. Vidya & Child offers a holistic approach through intensive training in life skills, arts and performing arts, along with academic, financial, and mentoring support. (www.vidyaandchild.org)

"Learning to read and write changes lives.
It means job, money, health and dreams fulfilled."
******

Vidya Poshak India

The heart of Vidya Poshak's (VP) philosophy lies in the slogan: Empower the Student Community. VP is a registered NGO, started in 2001 at Dharwad, Karnataka, by a group of philanthropists with the aim of supporting financially challenged but intellectually challenging students. It believes that investment in higher education provides significant dividends far beyond individual achievements and contributes to the overall betterment of society. It is a unique program that identifies bright students from economically disadvantaged families and nurtures them until they complete their higher education and has two established programs: a) Nurture Merit, which supports students from economically challenged backgrounds till they graduate and find suitable employment. b) Graduate Finishing School, an initiative to train economically disadvantaged graduates from rural areas in vocational skills. Students are provided library facilities, reference books, career counseling, free computer and internet access. Its development-based interventions help the student community to achieve their academic goals and to lead a standard professional and personal life, which ultimately leads to the effective progress of the nation as a whole. So far, the future of hundreds of graduates has been secured through gainful employment, which means freedom from the clutches of economic backwardness. (www.vidyaposhak.ngo)

"When girls are educated, their countries become stronger and more prosperous."
******

Wayanad Girijana Seva Trust

Baburaj and Rajeev reached Wayanad to take up jobs in their relevant careers, where they met a few Adivasis who came to town to shop for groceries. They were taken aback by what they heard and saw about the daily life struggles of the tribals. Driven by a desire to know more about their new friends, they forayed deep into the forests and reached some tribal villages and spent days and weeks with them to understand their concerns, distress, anxiety and ailments. Their penury, social insecurity, illiteracy, zero awareness of the world outside their dingy huts and their struggle for survival, shocked them beyond words. Men falling prey to alcohol, women being sexually abused and manipulated by immigrants from other parts of the State, the increasing number of unwed mothers, exploitation by government officials and land encroachers and more! Consequently, they became a minority in their own land. The children were the worst hit.

They lacked education as they had to become breadwinners at a very young age and were squeezed by their employers in countless ways.

Inspired by the continuous whisperings of Mother India- "They-are-also-my-children," Babu and Rajeev joined hands with a retired teacher, Raman Master and Wayanad Girijana Seva Trust was born in 2002. Babu and Rajeev resigned from their respective jobs and took up the mission to uplift the tribals and show them new paths to progress. As a prime step towards achieving this goal, the Trust started a Residential School with 42 children in a thatched shed and named it Vivekananda Residential Tribal Vidyalaya. Later, it was accredited with the National Institute of Open School of the HRD Ministry, Govt. India. Ever since, the trio, led by their conviction that every child has a right to education and a decent living, are full-time partners in the philanthropic project of bringing education to the children. Simultaneously, job-oriented training in tailoring and embroidery, bamboo crafting and computer literacy are also imparted to the students without disturbing their regular academic classes.

Adults too are taken care of. Evening classes in literacy, counseling sessions, training in needlework, carpentry and new techniques in farming are part of the adult curricula. Special classes are arranged for those above 18 years of age and are encouraged to attempt the matriculation equivalent exams. Knowing the worth of their services, NGOs like Paadhai, Care Foundation and Ramakrishna Mission helped to set up better infrastructure by joining hands with other like-minded Foundations. Now (2022), the school has a headcount of approximately 250 students. (www.wgstrust.org.in)

"No country can ever truly flourish if it stifles the potential of women and deprives itself of the contributions of half of its citizens (M. Obama)
******

Ammucare Charitable Trust

Ammucare is a registered non-profit organization established in India in 2003 by P.K Mohan, popularly known as Mohanji. The Trust was begun in the loving memory of his daughter Ammu, who, following a tragic road accident at the tender age of four flew to the Great Beyond on 23rd August 2000. During her brief sojourn on this planet, she touched the hearts of many through her radiance, pure love and maturity beyond her age. Ammu lives on through the smiles of the many who benefit through various selfless initiatives and acts of kindness undertaken by Ammucare Charitable Trust, which resonates with unconditional love and care beyond barriers. Ammucare provides food, shelter, clothing, medical care, education and other means of support to empower and uplift the helpless and the needy and paves the way to their growth and self-reliance. (www.ammucare.org)

"If you educate a girl today,
she will educate society every day."
******

Udaan India Foundation:

Mumbai-based Udaan's (Flight) mission is to provide timely and meaningful support to needy children, women, and senior citizens by effectively implementing projects in the area of health, education and nutrition, which have a sustainable, cost-effective and positive impact on society and environment. Started in 2004, the Foundation runs a one-year program in a secure and happy learning environment to facilitate school-readiness for children aged four to six from low-income communities. It aims to train the children in language and social skills. After kindergarten, they are supported through their school years till they become employable. (Email: udaanindiafoundation@gmail.com)

"The unfortunate need people who will be kind to them.
The prosperous need people to be kind to." (Aristotle)
******

Vanavil Trust

Started in the aftermath of the 2004 tsunami by a handful of youngsters, Vanavil (Rainbow) has grown with the help of individual donors and groups committed to the cause of education. It works closely with nomadic tribes such as Boom Boom Mattukaran and Narikuravar found in TN, who are neglected and under-served by the State. The mission of the Trust is to educate the children of these tribes and empower them. Its innovative educational model, nutritional support and livelihoods have created historic changes and development. Children enjoy personalized care and every child is assisted in getting a college degree, diploma or vocational training. (www.vanavil.org)

"It is not beyond our power to create a world in which all children have access to good education." (N. Mandela)

******

ATMA Foundation

ATMA Foundation, Thrissur, started by C.K. Suresh, a Professional Trainer, Life Guide and Relationship Coach, is a voluntary organization committed to empowering individuals and families and bringing about positive changes in the community. Over the years (2006-2022), it has organized very many programs, directly impacting hundreds of families. The Foundation's Vision speaks of creative intervention for social transformation through effective empowerment and productive compassion. The above Vision follows the mission of facilitating the blossoming of individuals and social groups to lead healthier lives with happier relationships and interpersonal harmony. It is a platform for people to find love and happiness for themselves and to spread it to the world around and works for individual empowerment, family welfare, community development, child protection, education, art and culture, disaster relief and rehabilitation, and more. (www.atmafoundation.org)

"Educating girl children is the best success mantra for India."

******

eVidyaloka

eVidyaloka (to educate anywhere-anytime) is an educational, social enterprise with a vision to ensure quality education for the children of rural India and was founded in January 2011 by Satish and Venkat, colleagues at Microsoft India, with the passion for bringing volunteerism and technology together. This Bengaluru-based NGO helps underprivileged children in far-off villages to get quality education through technology. It has benefitted umpteen children in over 200 remote villages, which has been achieved by connecting the children to volunteer teachers worldwide through live and interactive classes. Anyone interested can adopt a child from a remote village to give the child access to education and other life skills. (www.evidyaloka.org)

"Proper education can show
a brighter path for girls to go ahead."
******

E & H Foundation

Uttar Pradesh (UP) is the largest State in India, but its development lags behind the development targets fixed for the country. The State's Human Development Index (HDI) is one of the lowest compared to other States. E & H (Education &

Health) Foundation started its journey from Farrukhabad to lift the State from its educational backwardness and raise its health index. This Delhi-based organization works to ensure healthcare and quality education for underprivileged children in India through collaborative funding and field partnerships. Since its inception in 2012, E & H has reached 19,000 children in three districts of UP, belonging to the communities that are at the bottom of the socio-economic ladder, 80% of them being first-gen learners and over 50% being girls. The Foundation aims to reach 1,00,000 children by 2025. The Foundation focuses on children from Class I to Class X, with the conviction that every citizen in the country needs good quality education, at least till Class X, to be employed gainfully and to achieve her/his full potential in any field. The Foundation partners with the Gyan Shala (School for Knowledge) model that helps children achieve grade-appropriate learning in Classes I to IV. The organization has the active cooperation and support of committed individuals and corporate partners. (www.enhfoudation.in)

Kudos to NGOs that are doing non-profiting star-spangled performances in bringing quality education to the doorsteps of the disadvantaged and helping them to break out of the cycle of poverty.

Endnote:

India is steamrolling her way to greater heights in science and technology but illiteracy continues to plague a large section of Mother India's children. Education is a fundamental right of all citizens and not the privilege of a few. Promoting reading and providing access to books at a young age helps craft the personality of individuals, creates awareness, uplifts the downtrodden, and opens the way to fulfillment in life. Proper education helps to combat superstitious beliefs and alienation among people based on caste and creed, region and religion. What appears in the above pages is a drop in the mighty ocean of illiteracy. Let us hope that many such drops falling continuously from different parts of India will ultimately form the ocean of literacy and learning.

"A path to success, a safe ride to a secure future, a glue that joins our dreams and plans for sure, that shapes our character, promises a place in society; so, to climb the education ladder, let's be zesty."

******

Fight the battle with ignorance and misery
To set the captive children free.
May they continue to fight the battles of life
So their future will be secure and bright.

IV
MY HOME - MY CASTLE

A house is built with bricks and cement; it becomes a home when, with the brick of determination and the cement of love, the members move together to make life what it should be - a march towards togetherness and progress. A home is a place where love resides, family gathers, friends meet, memories are created and stored, where hope and laughter, tears and fears, wellness and illness, peace and frictions mingle freely, where Me for All and All for Me is the accepted norm. The happiness one experiences in achieving this feat is remarkable and indescribable in mere words. Then, for the home dwellers, even a hut becomes their Windsor Castle. Below are a few examples of how some caring humans heard the cry of the homeless and wiped their tears by providing them with a house to live in and making it a true home.

Eric Correa and Souharda Nagar

Eric Correa started his career on the lower rung of the socio-economic ladder and climbed the ladder of success with sheer hard work and the fearless pursuit of his dreams, the culmination of which was the realization of his dream of building and donating houses for the poor. It was a 2012 Republic Day Gift for the beneficiaries of Souharda Nagar - the colony of 34 houses located at Padumarnadu Village, Moodbidri, Dakshina Karnataka - as 34 families were handed over the keys of the houses built and donated to them by Eric Correa. The beneficiaries received the keys to their dream house from NRI businessman Ronald Colaço in a glittering inaugural ceremony in Souharda Nagar, held in the presence of many dignitaries. Among the beneficiaries in the new colony, there were Hindus, Muslims and Christians. Reiterating the importance of giving back to the society from which we have benefitted, Ronald Colaço said: "I am touched by this gesture of Eric, so I wanted to be a part of this important event. If a person having Rs.50,000/- donates Rs.5,000/-, his contribution is much greater than a person having Rs.50,00,000/- and donates Rs.50,000. On that count, Eric has overtaken many because his contribution comes to almost Rs.3,00,000,00/- in Souharda Nagar alone. What can be a greater donation than contributing more than 75% of one's savings as Eric did?" Ronaldo asked in wonderment and added that he would donate Rs.20,00,000/- for the 2nd project of Eric, which is being planned at Kodyadka, four km. from Souharda Nagar. Eric, the brain behind the entire project, spoke on the occasion, describing it: "An unforgettable event of my life." He said he could not have made his dream a reality but for the help of his mentors and friends.

He thanked Asif and Mohammed Sharif, from whom he bought the land. The new colony was blessed by Rev. Dr. Aloysius Paul D'Souza, Bishop of Mangalore Diocese, who pointed out that Eric Correa has set a good example for communal harmony by providing houses to the needy without discrimination on the grounds of race, language or religion.

Though Eric does not like his deeds to be highlighted in any media, he believes that his next venture of building 64 more houses for the poor at Kodyadka, Moodbidri (South Karnataka), could do with more helping hands. His work has inspired lovers of co-humans to extend their heartfelt support, both moral and financial, for 2nd and 3rd phases of the project. Eric, who has come up in a hard way, starting his career as an office boy and slowly graduating to have his own business, has set an inspiring example for others to emulate. (Details such as the date and place of birth of Eric, his family, education etc., are not available) (Daijiworld Media Network -Moodbidri 27.01.2012)

"At the end of the day, it's who you've lifted up, it's about what you've given back." (D. Washington)

******

Keerthi's Cry Resounded in Indira's Heart

Kattanam: There is no bond stronger and deeper than the bond between a mother and her child, though in one in a million cases, we find exceptions to the above claim. Here is one such example. At her birth, Keerthi's biological mother frowned at her and, without much ado, threw her into a waste bin. Why? The mother wanted a boy? Was Keerthi illegitimate? Sick? Deformed? Dark skinned? Not sure! Indira took the unwanted baby home and brought her up against heavy odds. Though Keerthi and Indira bonded well, Indira's family members gave her a tough time due to the unexpected addition to the family. Indira-Keerthi story was published in the Sunday Supplement of Manorama on 17 July 2016. After reading the story of the foster mother-daughter duo, many people of goodwill came forward to help Keerthi and her newfound mother. A house will be built for the twosome under the scheme Surakshitha Bhavanam Project (SBP, Secure Home Project) with the help of Kerala Action Force headed by Dr. Tony Fernandez, C.M. Haiderali and G.P. Charitable Trust. Film star Dilip will lay the foundation stone on 17 August 2016 and Keerthi and her foster mother Indira will shortly move to their new home, the first house under the SBP scheme. The house will have a space of 430 sq. ft.

with two bedrooms, a hall, a sit-out and a kitchen, costing Rs.5,50,000. The above-mentioned project plans to build 1000 houses for the roofless, with at least a few cents of land. (Manorama, 17.07.2016)

"It's not how big the house is;
it's how happy the home is."
******

Love Flowed from the Offering Box

Kazantzakis, the Greek Philosopher and writer, has written about a tree that flowered when asked to speak about God. The open offering box (*nercha petty*) of a Catholic Church in EKM Dt. flowered and spoke about God, the giver of all good things, by pouring out money into the lap of the helpless and the needy people of the area.

Here is how and when and where it happened! Demonetization created unprecedented problems - from the kitchen to the workplace, from school children's lunch boxes to medical care of the sick, from retail shop keepers to mega wholesalers and to everything connected with daily life. Millions of ordinary people were going from pillar to post to get enough money to meet the daily needs of their families. The unending queues in front of ATMs and bank counters showed no signs of relief anytime soon. After a few people who were struggling to meet their daily expenses confided in Fr. Jimmy Poochakkal, the Parish Priest of St. Martin's Church, Thevackal, the Church Committee took an unprecedented decision and the Vicar of the church made the unthinkable, love-laden announcement from the church, on Sunday during Holy Mass: "The offering box of the church will be kept open during the day and those who are in need of money could take the needed amount from the box and replace the same if and when the currency crisis is over and when they will have enough money to return the amount taken." The Sunday worshippers who heard the announcement pulled their ears and rubbed their eyes to make sure that they were not dreaming. True, for sure!

Following the announcement, devotees, irrespective of caste and religion, thronged to the church. About 200 families in the area benefitted from the generosity of the church. They used the money to buy items needed for survival - rice, groceries, vegetables, medicines, books, et al. The church authorities did not keep watch over who took what and did not keep an account of the money taken out of the offering box. Surprisingly, there were no takers for the currency notes of Rs.500/- and Rs.1000/- Trust begets trust! "People were facing a lot of difficulties due to demonetization. Many in the parish were struggling to buy daily necessities. A lot of them didn't know how to get their hard-earned cash from ATMs and banks. That was why we decided to open the donation boxes," Fr. Jimmy Poochakkal said. "Now the donation boxes are empty, but we are happy that we could give some relief to people when they faced a cash crisis," added Fr. Jimmy. In the Year of Mercy (December 2015 - November 2016) it was a proclamation of Mercy from the church at Thevackal. Such flowering of love and concern for others forces us to understand that it is one thing to be a human being, but being human is a different ball game. Let us believe that a bright future beckons us in spite of the umpteen heart-rending stories of the inhumanity of humans to other humans. (Manorama, 15.11.2016)

"If you're in the luckiest one percent of humanity, you owe it to think about the other 99 percent." (W. Buffett)

******

A Shepherd's Love-Gift to a Blind Couple

"There is no better way to thank God for your sight than by giving a helping hand to someone in the dark." We scarcely know how much of our pleasure and interest in life comes to us through our eyes until we are deprived of our ability to see. On 21 November 2016, Malayala Manorama, through its news column, called the attention of good-hearted Malayalees to the pathetic condition of the blind old couple Balakrishnan and Valsala, who were in search of a roof to protect them from the scorching sun and torrential rains. They heaved a sigh of relief when Cardinal Baselios Cleemis promised them a house of their own. During the Holy Mass at Christuraja Church, Munderi (near Gudalloor), the Cardinal called the attention of the faithful about the dire need of a safe roof for a sight-impaired couple and exhorted them to contribute generously towards the construction of a house. The request created positive vibrations in the giving hearts of a few and they responded generously. The Mass offerings received from the church and an addition of Rs.1,00,000/- will go for the construction of the house for Balakrishnan and Valsala. Dr. Joseph Mar Thomas, Bishop of Batheri also promised them his help. The house will be built on the four cents of land donated by the Vicar Fr. Mathews Vazhakoottathil of St. Mary's Orthodox Church,

Panamannu, Akampadam. When the Cardinal told the couple that all this is part of the providence of God, the couple confirmed it and said that they now believe in the providence of God more than ever; otherwise, such a big blessing in the form of a house would not have come their way. Cardinal Cleemis asked the couple to inform him when the house was completed and promised to be part of the blessing, *palu-kachal* ceremony and the opening of the house. (Manorama, 24.11.2016)

"The ache for home lives in all of us. It's a safe place where we can go as we are and not be questioned."

******

Sunil Responded to His Inner Call

"Life's persistent and the most urgent question is: What are you doing for others?" The above question, which Martin Luther King Jr. (1929-1964) asked more than half a century ago, rang a do-something-bell in the heart of Sunil Joseph Vanchickal, Thathampally, Alappuzha, after reading in Malayala Manorama about the miserable plight of Ashok Kumari and her children, a roofless family that made the premises of T.D. Govt. Medical College, Alappuzha, their home. The milk of human kindness spilt over from his heart and on listening to his inner voice, Sunil swung into action and decided that before celebrating the birth of Jesus, the Word made flesh in a stable, he would provide a home for the homeless flesh made in the world. He bought three and a half cents of land and a house in Kanjikkuzhi, Alappuzha and presented the same to Ashok Kumari and her children. On 25 December 2016, the birthday of the Homeless One, they left the premises of the hospital and took possession of a home of their own. The key to the new house was handed over to Ashok Kumari by the then Minister G. Sudhakaran, who requested the panchayat members to see to the continued security of the family. (Manorama, 27.12.2016)

"Amid pleasures and palaces though we may roam, Be it ever so humble, there's no place like home." (J.H. Payne)

******

Well Done Radha Jayan!

For parents of any caste or class, region or religion, the wedding of their daughter/son is certainly one of the happiest events of their life. However, Radha Jayan, a member of Kuttichal Panchayat, made this special day of her life extra special. In a rare display of compassion, Radha conducted the marriage of her financially weak neighbor Vijayan-Valsala couple's daughter Gita, along with her daughter Krishnaja's marriage and that too at the same venue. Yet more! Gita was offered gold ornaments and Rs.1,00,000/- as a wedding gift. While Ajayakumar, the son of Udayabhabu and Ambika of Vazhapally, took Krishnaja as his life partner, Anu, son of late Vishwanathan and Sujatha of Pulloorkonam Township House, Vizhinjam, joined his hands and heart with his bride Gita before witnesses and vowed to live together till death do them depart. Two weddings, one wedding hall, same *muhoortham* (auspicious time)and same food for all! People's representatives, including K S Sabarinathan MLA, participated in the function.

Valsala-Vijayan and Radha-Jayan were neighbors for almost two decades. Valsala works as a housemaid and also undertakes jobs provided under the National Rural Employment Guarantee Scheme. It was Radha who taught Valsala's daughter Gita, to read and write. She also taught her tailoring and helped her with the Std. X equivalency examination. It is this bond and love that prompted Radha to help Gita with her marriage. Years ago, Radha Jayan's name had filled the newspaper columns when the family donated pieces of land to six landless families whose only roof was the blue or dark sky with no safe place to lay their heads at night. Now, once again, Radha & Jayan are in the eye of the public and her name is circulating on social media once again. Radha Jayan is a resident of Chirakonam,

Ward X of Kuttichal Panchayat and is very actively involved in the social and financial problems of the people of her ward. (Mathrubhoomi.com 16.01.2017)

"Give what you have. To someone, it may be better than you dare to think." (Longfellow)

******

Gowrikuttyamma & K.E.College

"The difference between ordinary and extraordinary is that little extra," and Gowrikuttyamma, wife of the late Krishnan Nair of Naduvileparambil, Vazhappally, Changanassery possessed that little extra. Gowri was living in *Santhwanam*, a home for homeless women and children in Gandhi Nagar when she came to the aid of three other poor women who were inmates of the same institution. She divided 10.5 cents of land, which was all that she had in her name and donated it to these helpless women, including Radhamony, who couldn't cope with her drunken and wasteful husband and so left the house with her three children - Monisha, Mahesh and Manish. Mahesh and Manish lived in an orphanage in Ernakulam and Radhamony and Monisha were accommodated at Santhwanam. Radhamony did not have the wherewithal to build a house in the land received as a gift and Gowri was not in a position to help financially. Knowing that Monisha was an alumna of K.E. College, Mannanam, Anie Babu, the director of Santhwanam appraised the matter to the Principal Fr. Benny Thottanani. Under the leadership of the principal, the staff and students of the college raised Rs.6,50,000/- to construct the house. The transportation of building materials to the site was another challenge, as the piece of land was in a very remote area that no vehicle could reach. So the students of K.E. College and the inmates of Santwanam took up the role of head-load workers with no *nokku coolie* and carried the whole material needed for the house to the construction site. Construction work started in November 2016 and the house consisting of three bedrooms, hall and kitchen was completed in five months and was handed over to Radhamony and the children. Congratulations to the donor and to the construction workers! (Manorama, 10.04.2017)

"Everyone needs a house to live in, but a supportive family is what builds a home." (A. Liccione)

******

Not a Prey to the Glitter of Gold

History has many pages that are black with criminality and red with bloodshed perpetrated by the so-called civilized humans' inhuman behavior, which puts to shame even the beasts, all in the name of wealth in the form of gold, land or other valuables. But what happened in a village in Karnataka is an illuminating example of honesty. Located 100 km. from Bengaluru, Banasamudra in Malavalli Taluk of Mandya District has become the talking point in administrative and archaeological circles.

The story runs like this. The action unfolded when Lakshmamma (55) and a few laborers decided to resume digging the earth to lay the foundation stone for the house that Lakshmamma proposed to construct. As they continued digging, they found tiny coins covered with the mud that was being excavated. The laborers wanted to take the coins to a goldsmith but Lakshmamma decided to inform Halagur police. Inspector Sridhar, who heard about the discovery of the hidden treasure, rushed to the village and took 435 coins into custody. "Initially, we thought they were some beads. On cleaning them, we realized that they could be something precious from the past. Subsequently, we were told that they were gold coins," villagers recounted the incident to the district officials who reached the spot. Mandya Asst. Commissioner Arul Kumar said: "The total weight of the coins is 160 gms. Each coin has a unique design and is different from the others. Under the Karnataka Treasure Trove Act 1962, the coins were taken by the Tahsildar from the police and will be sent to the Archaeological department for examination." Narendra Swami, Malavalli MLA, told Times of India (ToI): "Handing over the hidden treasure is a pointer to the fact that truth and honesty still exist in this part of the State. Instead of being lured by the lucrative find, they chose to alert the government authorities." Swamy requested the govt. to study the coins and start the excavation of the area to ascertain its historical significance. (ToI, 19.05.2017)

"Better is a poor man who walks in his integrity than a rich man who is crooked in his ways." (Bible)

******

Anupriya Cycled into Our Hearts

The sun of goodness never sets! It shines ever! Any doubt? Read on! During the killer flood in 2018, Anupriya, the nine-year-old daughter of K.C. Shanmuganathan and Lalitha of K.K. Road, Villupuram, Tamil Nadu, decided to part with her four years' savings and donate the same towards the Chief Minister's Flood Relief Fund (CMFRF).

The little one had saved up to Rs.9000/- to buy her dream cycle. But when she watched on TV the visuals of the destruction caused by the flood in Kerala, her little heart melted in pity and she decided to help the flood victims in her own small way. "I had saved around Rs.9000/- for over four years to buy a cycle. But I saw the visuals of the Kerala flood on television and decided to give the money toward relief activities," she told reporters.

The story of this large-hearted Villupuram Little Great donor who broke open her piggy bank to contribute to the Flood Relief Fund was flashed across the State by social media. Instead of cycling to school, with her generous deed, Anupriya cycled into the hearts of Malayalees. Accolades, congratulations, appreciation, well-done wishes and more poured in. Hero Cycles Company's appreciation went beyond mere words.   On its official Twitter account, the company said: "Dear Anupriya, we appreciate your gesture to support humanity in the hour of need. You will get a brand-new cycle from us. Please contact us at customer@herocycles.com". Chairman and Managing Director of the Company, Pankaj M Munjal, hailed the little one: "Anupriya, pranam to you! You are a noble soul and may you spread the good around. Hero is pleased to give you one bike every year of your school life. Love you and best wishes! Prayers for Kerala!" Munjal said in a tweet.

Shashi Tharoor, Congress MP from Kerala, welcomed the company's gesture. "Thanks to Hero Cycles for donating a bicycle to a nine-year-old girl who gave up all that she was saving to buy a cycle to help the flood victims," he said in a tweet. Anupriya's father, Mr. Shanmuganathan, said that Manoj Kumar, the Sales Manager of Hero Cycles, had contacted them over the phone and lauded the little girl's gesture. The couple along with the child went to a cycle store in Villupuram, where Anupriya selected a blue Hero Sprint 2P. Well Done Anupriya! We are proud of you! (Manorama, 20.08.2018)

"We are the ones we've been waiting for.
We are the change that we seek." (B. Obama)
******

Manoj-Jayasree Duo on a Helping Mode

Dr. V K Manoj, an orthopedic surgeon in Dubai and his wife Jayasree Sebastian, a teacher at St. Mary's HSS, Kallanode, have decided to donate their one-acre plot on the banks of Kadantharapuzha at Chembanoda in Chakkittappara Panchayat to 14 families in memory of their grandfather Illickal Kunjouseph, who was a known philanthropist. The beneficiaries include three students from St Mary's HSS, where Jayasree teaches. The couple said: "We have been thinking about this for a while and were in the long process of identifying eligible families. Our relatives, friends and panchayat officials helped us in our search for deserving families. The chosen families do not own a house or possess a piece of land, nor do they get any benefit from the government."

Manoj-Jayasree couple has three children: Ashikh Kurian Manoj (Engineer in Dubai), Annu Manya Manoj (a student at NIT-C), Aardra Rose Manoj (a Class V student at Pazhassiraja Universal Public School). "When the idea struck us, we discussed it with our children, who readily agreed to it," said Jayasree. "We will try our best to help find sponsors to build houses for the families. Two of our friends have already expressed their willingness. Our idea is to construct environment-friendly houses which can withstand natural calamities," she added. The family will hand over all the documents of the land to the Minister for Labour and Excise, T. P. Ramakrishnan, at a function to be held at Peruvannamuzhi on 24 September 2018. (TNIE 18.09.2018)

Manager Susheela Managed Well!

A family that was on the verge of losing its house owing to a loan default never thought the very same bank officials who had come to attach its mortgaged property would become its savior. The manager and officials of the Pandalam branch of Kerala Bank who came across the plight of Rajamma and her three unmarried siblings who live at Thonnalloor at Elassery decided to do their bit so that the hapless family got back their land in which stands their unfinished house. Battling a similar experience in her childhood, the bank Manager K. Susheela could easily empathize with Rajamma. "I joined the Pandalam branch of the bank as its Manager in November 2020. While examining the files of default loans, I stumbled upon the case of this family who had pledged their property against a loan of Rs.1,00,000/- on 30 May 2008 to construct a modest house," said Sushhela.

The three-member family that lived by doing odd jobs was at the bottom of the financial ladder and hence their dream house remained in the realm of dreams and the construction work of the house was almost at a standstill. Matters moved from bad to worse when the makeshift shelter where the family was temporarily residing was gutted. The bank initiated recovery proceedings on 04

November 2010 when the arrears due to the default in payments came to the tune of Rs. 2,50,000. The amount was brought down to Rs.1,28,496/- at a bank *adalat*. "I visited their property site as part of the recovery procedures and was moved by the pathetic state of affairs of the family. I was determined to help them out to prevent the bank from taking over the property," said Susheela. "What came as a blessing was our WhatsApp group composed of the banking community which includes retired officials as well. I presented the case of the family in the group. The response was so overwhelming that contributions started pouring in. My husband and children supported me and willingly chipped in. In a few days I was able to pool in Rs.99,000. Hence, through a collective effort, the principal amount was repaid fully and the family was happy to get back their property on 31 March." The property documents were handed over to the family. Three cheers to Ms. Susheela and team who scripted a noble deed and thus saved a debt-ridden family! (Manorama 13.04.2021)

"It is every man's obligation to put back into the world at least the equivalent of what he takes out of it." (A. Einstein)

******

A Super-Active Heart in an Inactive Body

Gandhian principles were deeply rooted in Thomas Pallipurayidam of Kanjikuzhi Panchayat, Idukki, even as a student at Newman's College, Thodupuzha. When the college took over the govt.'s housing scheme, as the Secretary of the NSS unit of the college, Thomas played a vital role in completing the project, which secured him the adulation of many and the college received recognition from the govt. in the form of *puraskars*. At present, Thomas is not very active physically due to illnesses of all kinds, but his heart is ever active when it comes to helping someone in need. When the 2018 flood swallowed up the life and living of many people, Thomas and his family understood the helplessness and pain of those who have no roof to call their own. Today, six of these roofless and helpless families live in safe houses of their own because Thomas, who owned only 125 cents of land, handed over 30 cents to the diocese of Idukki, which the diocese handed over to the Collector. The soil was tested and found fit for building and with the help of the govt., six love-nests came up where six families live happily now.

Thomas was working as a representative of a medical company at EKM when his kidneys started a non-cooperation movement, which forced him to leave his job. His wife, who was working as a designer in the medical company, was forced to give up the job because her presence was needed at home to look after her sick husband. Moreover, to meet the hospital expenses, he had to sell his house and land in EKM. He keeps himself alive today with regular dialysis at Taluk Hospital, Thodupuzha. Even when his body is weak and helpless, he continues to do his share to reduce the sufferings of others in whichever way he can. (Deepika, 07.01.2019)

"No one is useless in this world who lightens the burdens of another." (C. Dickens)

******

Nias Bharathi Gives . . . Gives

"Whatever you do to the least of my brothers, you do to me." Here is Nias Bharathi, who translated into practice the above words of the bible. Nias, who hails from Kilimanoor, TVPM, started his journey on the path of altruism when he heard about a homeless four-year-old living with his grandmother after he was abandoned by his mother. His first act of generosity was in favor of Bencylal of Chirayinkeezhu, to whom he donated four cents of land. Later, he collected the names of landless people from the related govt. office and added a few more names to the category of the landless. From this list, he chose ten deserving persons, which included widows, physically or mentally challenged, orphans, those abandoned by their husbands and so on. In the third week of January 2019, it was decided to hand over the necessary documents to the chosen beneficiaries, who have to give an undertaking in writing that for the next 15 years, the land will not be sold or transferred to anyone.

He is planning a village to be named Gandhiji Village, founded on Gandhian values and all-inclusiveness. The village will have a nursery, reading room, place of worship, rainwater tank, waste disposal unit and more to be completed in two years' time. "At the end of the day, we do not carry anything from this earth when death comes calling," said Nias. " So why not share what you have with those who have nothing?" Definitely not just a philosophical question but one that is down-to-earth and practical. *Magnanimous, Munificent Nias!* (Deepika, 07.01.2019)

"When a man dies, he carries within his clenched hands only that which he has given away." (Rousseau)

******

St. Stephen School's Own Malavika

"I am very happy to have a new home," that was all Malavika could say. The 12-year-old Malavika from Kuttampuzha Panchayat, Kothamangalam, was a student of St. Stephen's HSS, Keerampara. Her sad plight came to the attention of the school authorities when the famished Malavika burst into tears while on the school bus heading towards the school. Her father, Subramanyam, was rendered jobless after the 2018 floods and her polio-affected mother could not do much towards family income. Following a report by The Hindu about Malavika's sad plight, her teachers visited her place and were shocked to see the pitiful conditions in which she lived. They formed a WhatsApp group to raise funds to build a house for her. Students, teachers, the school PTA and a few locals opened their hearts and their purses. Eventually, the Malavika House Fund touched Rs.6,75,000. A compassionate resident donated three cents of land which was on an elevated region with no direct access to the road. So, transporting the building materials to the site was a herculean task. With the willpower and the good-heartedness of everyone concerned - principal, teachers, students, locals - the dream house was materialized and was handed over to the family in July 2020. (The Hindu, 15.07.2020)

Binu Thomas Gave of What He Had

"Extraordinary times call for extraordinary measures." But Binu Thomas, a 46-year-old former Block Panchayat member, did not think that he was doing anything extraordinary during the extraordinary times when COVID-19 brought the world to its knees. "I am doing my bit in the fight against this dreaded disease," said Binu. "The sad faces of the COVID-19 victims in my neighborhood family flashed through my mind. The head of the family died the previous day. The family had to wait for 48 hours to get a slot at the public crematorium. I made up my mind and said YES to the idea of giving up my land to be used as a crematorium," Binu recalled. But initially, the inspiration came from Shibu, a ward member who suggested to Binu to part with his land on the secluded Mukkunnimala hilltop, which is part of Pallichal Panchayat, to set up a temporary crematorium for COVID-19 victims. Vilavoorkal and Pallichal Panchayats were among the several Local Self Govt. bodies in the State struggling to find a suitable place to cremate the bodies of those who bowed to the merciless attack of COVID-19. Public crematoriums at Maranalloor, Nedumangad and Santikavadam, owned by the TVPM Corporation, were the only options for these two panchayats. Binu and Shibu, who were part of the Rapid Response Team of Vilavoorkal Panchayat for Covid Prevention and Control activities, felt the urgent need for a crematorium. So, Binu signed an agreement with Vilavoorkal and Pallichal Panchayats, allowing them temporary possession of his 66-cent plot, where the locals would be permitted to cremate the bodies of COVID-19 victims until the pandemic said goodbye. I.B. Satheesh, Kattakada MLA, hailed Binu's act as inspiring and worthy of imitation by those who look only for their own comforts and gains. (Indian Express, 12.05.2021)

"No act of kindness, no matter how small, is ever wasted."
(Aesop)
******

A House for Kavitha

Kavitha studied in St. Joseph's, Alappuzha, from the Nursery to PDC. After her marriage at the age of 26, she waited for 14 years to hold her bundle of joy, a baby girl, who was named Athidhi. A few months before the baby opened her eyes to the wonders of this world, Kavitha's husband abandoned her. When her in-laws realized that the newborn was a victim of autism, the mother-baby duo were kicked out of the house. Ever after Kavitha was living with her aged mother Saraswathy (84) and differently-abled Athidhi (7) in a rented house near Kommady toll gate and working as a last-grade staff in Sanjo Hospital, Alappuzha, when it was discovered that the killer cancer had taken up its residence in her body. Chemotherapy, injections, surgery, et al., followed at the Govt. Hospital, Alappuzha. Subsequently, her left breast was removed. Later the merciless, villainous cancer established its sovereignty on her left thigh bones too.

The retired staff of St. Joseph's College for Women, Alappuzha - who has a post-retirement *Koottayma* (fellowship) known as Golden Agers - came to know about Kavitha's sad plight in November 2021 through a few Josephian alumnae. Comments like: Kavitha is our own; we must help her, passed on from mouth to mouth - nay - from heart to heart among the Golden Agers. A few of them used various communication media to appraise the alumnae and the present staff about the pitiable condition of Kavitha. Soon enough, Josephian Golden Agers, present staff, alumnae and a few well-wishers joined hands and a house worth Rs.13,00,000/- was purchased and registered in Kavitha's name and the key of the house with two bedrooms, kitchen, toilet, sit out et al was handed over to her on 25 January 2022, while clicking cameras, social and print media reporters were conspicuous by their absence. About Rs.1,00,000/- was deposited in her bank account for further treatment. Athidhi was admitted to Santhwan, a school for special children managed by the Diocese of Alappuzha, where she is learning to read and write, sing and dance, paint and draw and other skills needed to live. (St. Joseph's Convent, Alappuzha, 25.01.2022)

"The most truly generous persons are those who give silently without hope of praise or reward." (C. R. Brink)

******

Nilan C/O Advika C/O Nilan

Nilan Krishnan was born a girl; later, she became a boy. Advika was born a boy; as he grew up, he became she. The two, who had been in a relationship for some time, decided to fly against the headwind of alienation and get married at the Thiru-Kachamkurissi temple in Palakkad, Kerala. "We want to prove that in spite of the social discrimination, unfavorable judgment and mockery about our abilities and God-given talents, we have a right to have a family and occupy our allotted space on this planet," they said. But they were in for a shock when they printed the wedding invitation where the above temple was mentioned as the venue of the ceremony. Many who fall into this group co-exist in close quarters, but the ceremony of getting married and formally declaring to be lifetime partners is a rare event.

The temple authorities denied permission to perform the ceremony in the temple premises. So, they were forced to move the function to a nearby hall.

Isha Kishore, a transgender activist, termed the incident unfortunate because the couple's request to get married in the temple area was rejected solely based on their gender. She said: "Every temple has its own set of laws and ceremonies and I absolutely agree with that. However, in this instance, they refused permission based on gender. Everyone in this universe, in my opinion, is the Almighty's creation. Hence, how can the temple administration forbid the couple from entering God's house on account of their gender?" The temple officials, who are a part of the Malabar Devaswom Board, refuted the allegation: "Not the couple, but someone else related to them came here and notified us of the plan of Nilan and Advika to get married in the temple. We were unaware that the pair belonged to the transgender community. No such marriage had ever taken place in the temple. We do not permit love marriages which take place without the consent of the parents and other close relatives because such weddings could lead to future legal problems and police investigations."

While accusations, discussions and debates over the issue filled the air and flew off in different directions, the wedding of Nilan and Advika took place in the presence of their supportive families and a good number of well-wishers in Shekundhar Marriage Hall, Kollangode, in the Nenmara Constituency of the Palakkad District. Thus, they scaled the wall of social boycott and alienation that was considered high and un-scalable. The event was proof that we as a community can and should accept one and all as members of the human family, no matter what the gender and social status of a given person is. Nilan Krishan, a trained Lab Technician and Advika, an Operation Theatre Technician, are employed in the sales section of Finmart. *We salute you Nilan and Advika! Wish you a life of self-fulfillment!* (Manorama, 25.11.2022)

> *"A house is made of bricks and beams.*
> *A home is made of hopes and dreams."*
> ******

Gold Ear-Rings, Bronze Medal, House

S. Sonia had mortgaged her only precious property - her gold earrings - to meet the expenses of participating in the 3000 mt. walk, which was part of the State School Sports Meet, 2022. She missed her gold earrings but brought home a Bronze Medal. Meanwhile, Sonia's family was given notice by the Indian Railways to vacate the no-man's land where they were living in a hut. The newspapers and social media took up the case and flashed across the State the sorry plight of a State School Sports Medal Winner. Reading about Sonia and her family's miserable plight, A.K. Narayanan, Ayilyam House, Koduvayur, Palakkad Dt. reached their hut and promised to get a new house for them. Narayanan, who possesses a giving heart, had earlier given houses to four roofless families who live in and around Koduvayur and Elevancherry. The gold earrings that were mortgaged were retrieved and handed over to Sonia by Sevabharathi.

Following the death of her father, Sonia, her brother Sohan and their mother, Priya, are living with Priya's parents. But life is not all sunshine and sugar for them. Sonia's maternal grandparents, Shashi and Sathyabhama, are heart patients. As Priya has to be at home to take care of her ailing old parents, she cannot go out to take up a job.

Sonia, by her hard work and perseverance, won a bronze medal, earrings and now a house. Stay Blessed, Sonia! May your hands be stretched out to help the needy in return for the help you received! (Manorama, 12.12.2022, B'lore ed.)

"No one has ever become poor by giving" (Anne Frank)

******

Arsha & Ardra Are Smiling

Five years ago, the killer cancer claimed their mother, Salila. Not long after, the father of the family became a victim of severe heart problems and said his final goodbye to his two daughters, Arsha and Ardra. Arsha (23) was born with deformed legs that are unable to carry her around, so she moves on an electric wheelchair that was gifted to her by the Jana-maithri Police (People-friendly Police) of Haripad. With the departure of both parents, the future of the two girls remained a big question mark. Though physically challenged in many ways, Arsha was determined to live by the fruits of her labor and help her sister Ardra, a Class VIII student of N.S.S. Girls' High School, Karuvatta, to finish her studies, which alone would open her a door to safe employment and decent living.

Following a report by Malayala Manorama highlighting the pathetic condition of the girls living in Kumarapuram of Alappuzha Dt., a few helping hands came forward to lift the sisters from the pit of problems to the height of possibilities and pave a safe path for them to move on in life. When the district administration joined hands with the Rotary Club, their wishes and dreams were transformed into reality. Arsha expressed her wish to begin an Online Service Centre. Without much delay, a room attached to their house was ready and a laptop, printer, photostat machine, table, chair and so on were brought in and soon Arsha was tip-toeing with Online Service. Ardra cycles to and from school, thanks to the generosity of well-wishers. The Social Justice Dept. of the State sanctioned Rs.1,50,000/- towards further improvement of Arsha's online service and Ardra's academic career. *Good Luck, Arsha, Ardra! Life Beckons You! Move on!* (Manorama, 16.02.2023)

"Our unselfish efforts to bring cheer to others will be the beginning of a happier life for ourselves." (H. Keller)
******

Rituraj is the Raja of His House

For the past few days, the classmates of Rituraj Std. X student of S.N. Trust HSS, Nattika, Thrissur Dt. have been wondering why Ritu had become so silent and sad. Finally, they questioned him: "What's the matter, bro? Why is this silence?" Ritu opened up and uncloaked his concern about his study and future. His family's only possession, a leaky old house, had been mortgaged in 2014 for Rs.1,25,000/- at the Village Development Bank, Thrippayar Branch, Chavakkad. Ritu's father, Mohanan, was employed in a workshop. When the mega Covidian tragedy was engulfing the State, like many other victims of cruel Covid, Mohanan lost his job. To add to it, his mother met with an accident that needed expensive medical care. So, the family was forced to call a halt to their installment-based payback of the loan. Now, adding interest upon interest, the amount to be repaid had risen to Rs.2,22,000/- and Ritu understood that there was no way to find the money within the stipulated period and the end would be that the bank authorities would attach his house. Ritu, who always dreamt of a decent house to live in, was in despair. Since the property documents were in the bank, his family could not make use of the Life Mission Project of the State Govt.

Ritu's friends were not prepared to hear his story, forget it and go back to their routine school days. From his concerned friends, the school authorities heard about Ritu's predicament and they acted to get back the usual smile on his face. His teachers and friends contacted the bank and asked for three months' time to repay the loan in one installment. Under the leadership of NSS Programme Co-ordinator Shalabha Shankar, the big-hearted teachers and students worked in unison. They undertook the Biriyani Challenge, Lottery Tickets Challenge, Hand-wash & Dish-wash Challenge and more challenges. Within the stipulated three months' time, their concerted efforts produced the desired result and their purse whispered: "Enough." Finally, Ritu's property document left the darkness of the bank locker and was handed over to meet the sunshine faces of Rituraj and his parents. *Hai! New-gen Bros, the future of our country is safe in your hands!* (Manorama, 23.02.2023)

"We can't help everyone, but everyone can help someone."
(R. Reagan)
******

From a Rented House to Ente Veedu

Chittilappilly-Mathrubhoomi *'Ente Veedu'* (My House) Project is a mission to build 1,000 houses for the roofless. K. Chittilappilly Foundation Chairman Kochouseph Chittilappally and Mathrubhoomi Managing Director M.V. Shreyams Kumar officially declared the project at the inaugural function held in Ernakulam in April 2022. Under the project worth Rs.40 crore, houses will be built and presented to 1000 deserving families selected from different districts. By the end of April 2022, 13 beneficiaries were selected and Rs.52,00,000/- were granted for the first phase of the project, and Rs.4,00,000/- each will be handed over to the beneficiaries. The housewarming of the first beneficiary who completed the construction of the house was held on 19 May 2022 at Vythiri in Wayanad. Kochouseph Chittilappilly urged everyone to contribute her/his share for the welfare of society and pointed out that the government is not the only agency responsible for wiping out poverty from the State. Addressing the event, M.V. Shreyams Kumar stated that 'Mathrubhoomi' is always committed to taking up similar socially responsible projects to benefit our suffering co-humans.

Bavitha, her husband Jayachandran and daughter Aaradhya have been living in a rented house for the last 12 years, always dreaming of the day when they will have a roof of their own. So, Bavitha and her family could not contain their joy when they received the key to their new home, jointly constructed by 'Mathrubhoomi' and K Chittilappilly Foundation as part of the 'Ente Veedu' Project, which works to realize the day when there will be no one in God's Own Country without a roof of her/his own. This is the third house under the Kannur Unit of the project. Handing over the key to the family, Minister K Radhakrishnan said, "Ente Veedu initiative is a model for others and such good deeds of voluntary organizations, joining hands with the State Government's dream of everyone having Ente Veedu, are appreciable." Meanwhile, Bavitha and the team, with tears of joy flowing freely from their cheeks, expressed their gratitude towards Mathrubhoomi and the Chittilappilly Foundation for making their dream come true. (Mathrubhoomi, 23.02.2023)

On 12 May 2023, Mathrubhoomi reported that the key to the 50th house under the Ente Veedu Project was handed over to T. Shiny, a widow and mother of two children, of Kavilumpara Panchayat, Kozhikode.

Parinayam @ Rotary District 3211

It is 26 February 2023. As the Camelot Convention Centre, Pathirapally, Alappuzha, glittered with serial bulbs and colorful decorations and the clicking sound of the cameras reverberated unceasingly, tears of joy flowed freely from the eyes of 28 differently abled couples while their hearts beat in unison with gratitude and expectation as they were united in wedlock at a social wedding ceremony held at the above center. Groom T. Shaji from Kurumbala, Panthalam and Bride M.K. Bhasura from Maliekkal House, Kuttanad, are visually impaired. Groom P. Shaji, Shyamala Bhavan TVPM and Bride A. Sheeja, Anchal, Kollam are in wheelchairs. Groom Christopher Manchumalayil, Vandiperiyar and Bride Dhanya, Malayil House, Vazhakulam, Moovattupuzha, are physically challenged. These and 25 more specially challenged, during a ceremony titled Parinayam (Malayalam word for wedding) tied the knot under the aegis of Rotary International District 3211 on 26 February 2023 at Camelot Convention Centre, Alappuzha. The newlyweds hailed from TVPM, Kollam, Kottayam, Pathanamthitta and Alappuzha districts. Apart from meeting the expenses of the wedding, all the couples were provided with one sovereign gold chain, Rs.25,000/- and furniture needed for their homes. The Rotary Club will supply food items for the next six months. More than 1,110 Rotarians who are in the field of industry and business will take the initiative to find fitting employment for them depending on their qualifications and training in various skills. Others will be trained to undertake any income-producing jobs. A.M. Arif MP, P.P. Chitharanjan MLA, V.R. Krishna Teja, Collector, K. Babumon Rotary District Governor and many other dignitaries present showered blessings and good wishes on the newlyweds. (The Hindu, Manorama, Deepika & Mathrubhoomi, 27.02.2023)

> *"Call it a clan, call it a network, call it a tribe, call it a family. Whatever you call it, whoever you are, you need one."* (J. Howard)

800 Marriages @ Sunni Yuvajana Sangham

"I couldn't hold my tears on seeing such a wonderful moment. Emotions of fulfillment and communal harmony overwhelmed me and thousands of others who witnessed the event," said Jamat Karulai, District Secretary of the Kerala Muslim Jamat. But what was that highly emotionally charged moment? Here it is! As many as 800 young women and men tied the knot and promised to live together till death do us part at a mass wedding organized by Sunni Yuvajana

Sangham (SYS) on the premises of the Padanthara Markaz, at Padanthoral, near Gudalur on Sunday, 26 February 2023. The event held at this small village on the Tamil Nadu-Kerala border has been hailed as a fine example of all-embracing communal harmony. As many as 74 brides and grooms who were married at the function were non-Muslims. Their marriage rites took place at the neighboring Muthumariyamman temple and a church. Devarshola Abdussalam Musliar, who organized the event, was acclaimed as the hero of the day and was covered with shouts and songs: Congratulations! Well Done!! Do-it-again!!! Apart from clothes and other personal expenses, five sovereigns of gold were given to each couple. "Philanthropists from different parts helped us conduct the community wedding," said the Musliar. The event marked the 30th anniversary of the Padanthara Markaz. Samastha Kerala Jamiyyathul Ulama President E. Sulaiman Musliar presided over the function and Syed Ali Bafaqui Thangal led the prayer. Top leaders of the Kerala Muslim Jamat, including A.P. Aboobacker Musliar and Abdul Khader Musliar, greeted the newlyweds. If the reader has any lingering doubt about Kerala's tagline: God's Own Country, throw your doubt into the Arabian Sea. Kerala is God's Own and God's Zone. (The Hindu, 28.02.2023)

An Extraordinary Jubilee Celebrations

Ramzan Mahal, Royapuram, Chennai, had a festive look on 08 March 2023. Serial bulbs, decorations, music, Hello! Hello! Hai! Hai! Broad smiles more. Why such festivities? Under the auspices of the All Kerala Muslim Cultural Centre (AKMCC), 17 pairs of brides and grooms belonging to Hindu, Christian and Muslim communities pronounced the marriage vows - the couples had the freedom to follow the rituals of their own religion - and entered into a lifelong partnership, in riches and poverty, in sickness and health, in sorrow and joy, till death claimed them. Each couple was given 10 gm. gold and household articles costing about Rs.1,50,000/-. The event was the first bell of the Muslim League Platinum Jubilee Celebrations. A total of 75 such marriages are on the to-do list of the celebration committee. Panakkad Syed Sadiqali Shihab Thangal inaugurated. Muslim League National President K.M. Khader Moideen presided. Syed Sadiqali Shihab Thangal of Panakkad said that it was a historic event in the 75th year of the Muslim League that it was possible to get 17 couples to marry on International Women's Day. Platinum Jubilee celebrations of the Indian Union Muslim League started today with the tagline: 75 Years of Responsible Politics.

Basheer and His Fleet-Footed Team Did It

Inspector Baheer Chirackal was on duty during the *pooram* celebrations at Bhagavathy Temple, Kannenkavu, Malappuram Dt, when he was told that his school classmate Nirmala lives in the same area. Basheer paid her a visit with the hope of taking a happy trip down memory lane with his teenage friend, but it turned out to be an eye-opener for him. He found Nirmala living in an about-to-be-blown-off hut. After a short chit-chat and laughter, he left the place with a determination to do something for Nirmala, for old-time's sake.

Basheer and Nirmala were classmates during their school days at Mukkala High School, Marancherry. At the end of the school days, almost as a routine, promises such as - will never forget you, will keep in touch were given and taken with great enthusiasm and sincerity. Thereafter as circumstances would have it, each took different routes to secure their future. Meanwhile, Basheer had heard that Nirmala had gone abroad in search of greener pastures. So, he took it for granted that Gulf-returned Nirmala is living in the upper echelon with her hard-earned money. But what he saw was a different story. Nirmala ended her Marunadan life and returned home with an empty purse and the unpaid heavy debts that she incurred prior to her flight to the land of golden dreams. When teary-eyed Nirmala related her thwarted foreign pursuit, Basheer resolved to do something concrete to prove the worth of his friendship. He contacted a number of his old school friends. They opened their willing hearts and ready hands and said: "Yes, we will get a house ready for Nirmala." Done! A 650 sq. ft. house was ready without many roadblocks in a short time. On 21 May 2023, Nirmala and her family shifted to their new Castle, thanks to Basheer and his expeditious, ever-ready friends. Google says: Basheer means one who brings good news. *Congrats, Inspector Basheer! You brought more than good news to Nirmala!* (Mathrubhoomi, 22.05 2023)

"Turn the key; walk through the door.
This new house is all you ever wanted and more."
******

Tomy-Tom Alliance for a Good Cause

"Our most valuable possessions are those which can be shared without lessening, those which, when shared, multiply." Not sure whether Tomy Michael of Edakkom, Kannur, had ever come across this quote but he practiced it without much fanfare and without the ever-present and everywhere present social media's celebratory comments like: Well Done Tomy & Tom! You are a Wonderful Team! The land measuring one acre and 8.5 cents which Tomy, together with his sister's husband Tom Francis, bought for Rs.25,00,000/- was distributed to 11 families who till then didn't have the joy of possessing a piece of land on our planet. The land with electricity and water connections is about one km. away from the town of Edakkom.

Tomy, who retired from the Federal Bank, is a State Committee Member of the Bank Employees Federation of India and his wife Silvy is a retired teacher and Tom Francis is a native of Edoor. While Tomy was the Zonal Convenor of the Initiative for Rehabilitation and Palliative Care (IRPC), he had spent hours listening to the pathetic stories of the landless citizens of Kannur. Just listening and doing nothing, not bothering about the afflictions of the landless, was not the philosophy of Tomy. Now Tomy-Tom duo has switched on their search engine to find benign humanitarians who will be willing to loosen their purse strings and contribute towards building love-nests for these 11 families. Soon, these once landless-roofless families will have a safe habitation. (Mathrubhoomi, 10.06.2023)

"A man's true wealth is the good that he does in this world."
******

A Worthy Retirement Memorial

Much before his retirement day, Reji Mathew, Kizhakkekandam, a teacher in Vocational HSS, Muthukulam, Alappuzha, had heard about the stressful situation of Shalini Samuel of Pathiyoor, Alappuzha, who did not have a roof to call her own. So, on 31 May 2023, the day he retired and said goodbye to his teaching career, he also said Welcome to Shalini by his magnanimous deed. He handed over the necessary documents of 3.5 cents of land that was in his name, to Shalini through Joshua Mar Ignathios, the Bishop of the Syro-Malankara Catholic Diocese, Mavelikara. On the following day, 01 June 2023, the foundation stone of the dream castle of Shalini was laid in the gifted land that is along the Pandavarkavu-Ramapuram road. Under the guidance of Bishop Joshua and with the help of a few supportive hands, a modest house for Shailni will take shape in the near future. *Stay Blessed, Reji Mathew! May you continue your ministry of caring and sharing!* (Manorama, 02.06.2023)

"Helping others is the secret sauce to a happy life."
(Todd Stocker)
******

Endnote:

What is a home? Oxford Dictionary answers: "The place where one lives permanently, especially as a member of a family or a household." A structure built to accommodate a few people can be called a house. A home is built not with bricks or wood but with familial love and understanding among the parents and siblings. Home is more than a place; it is a feeling of contentment and happiness that the members share with the ones they love. Moreover, home is where one knows they are with people who can drive them insane in a second, and the same people can make them feel like rising stars the next second as well. A person could be at the height of material prosperity, but it would mean nothing if he/she did not have someone to share it with.

Having said this, we remember world citizens like Swamy Vivekananda, Dr. APJ Abdul Kalam, and A.B. Vajpayee, who did not have a blood-related family but adopted their country - nay the world - as their family and treated all human beings as their brothers and sisters with whom they shared what they had.

Beyond compare is my castle, my home
Where I am wanted, loved and freely roam.
Home, where care & share are the norms
Where fights & flights, love & laughter
easily foam.

Let's start now to laugh often and much
To win the respect of intelligent people
And the affection of children
To earn the appreciation of honest critics
And to endure the betrayal of false friends
To appreciate beauty, to find the best in others
To leave the world a bit better
Whether by a healthy child, a garden patch
Or a redeemed social condition
To know even one life has breathed easier
Because you have lived!
This is to have succeeded. (R.W. Emerson)